בס"ד

Joyfully Jewish — volume One

Create Your Joyfully Jewish Life

A 30 DAY STEP-BY-STEP WORKBOOK AND CREATIVE JOURNAL

Rae Shagalov

Contact the author or publisher.
E-mail: info@holysparks.com

- For wholesale discounts and bulk discounts for bookstores, groups and teachers

- To arrange a creative workshop or author event with Rae Shagalov

- For custom calligraphy or Artnotes from classes, live or recorded

- To dedicate a volume in the Joyfully Jewish series
  in memory or honor of someone special

Printed in the United States of America
First Printing 2018
ISBN: 978-1-937472-05-4 paperback

Holy Sparks Press
WWW.HOLYSPARKS.COM

Los Angeles

Tu Beshvat 5778

Please do not color on Shabbat or Jewish holy days
as writing and coloring are prohibited by Jewish law on those days.

This is a gift for:

From:

May you be blessed with success and only good things

These Hebrew letters appear at the top of each Artnotes page:

בס"ד

This is an abbreviation for the Aramaic phrase "B'Siyata Di'Shamaya,"
which means, "With the Help of Heaven."

OR

בי"ה

This is an abbreviation for Baruch Hashem (Blessed is the Name of G-d)

Putting these letters at the top of every page reminds us
that everything comes from G-d.

❧ ARTIST'S NOTE ☙

"Any mistakes contained herein are my own. Although my Artnotes artistically
capture some of the deep insights of the teachers, my Artnotes cannot convey
the warmth, caring, humor, incredible stories and intellectual challenge you will
experience when you attend Torah classes in person."

In this Joyfully Jewish Journey, you'll get fun, creative tools you can use
to grow in Torah & mitzvahs, and become calm, happy, energized, and focused.
With G-d's help, you'll get CLEAR-MINDED about what to do next so
that you can be pleasantly productive and delightfully on track in your life.

You'll get tips and techniques from Torah and Chassidus, and beautiful
calligraphy Artnotes & coloring pages to help you reduce the stress and
pressure of your life. You'll also have guided meditations to help you
eliminate stress while you strengthen your faith and your connection to G-d.

Each adventure in this Soul Journey only takes 5 - 10 minutes (with
a few longer mini-retreats) so you won't be overwhelmed (promise!).
Most importantly, you'll have a PLAN you can use whenever you feel
overwhelmed so that you won't get lost in the whirl and spin of your busy
life anymore.

You won't feel alone. You'll feel happy, supported, and excited to be focused
on your mission and in everything you do.

So, are you ready? Let's get started!

❧ CONTENTS ❧

I love being Jewish! But I didn't always. In fact, I left Judaism for 10 years and became a "spiritual tourist." You see, when I was growing up, I never learned about the spiritual secrets of authentic Torah. I thought there was no such thing as Jewish meditation or Jewish spirituality. I didn't even think Jews were supposed to be happy! Then, through developing my craft as a calligrapher, I discovered the mystical secrets of Judaism. When I began to explore the Alef Bet, letter-by-letter, the holy Hebrew letters led me on a quest to discover a deep, soulful, joyful Judaism I never knew existed.

By the grace of G-d, from the very beginning of my Torah learning I discovered my talent as a Jewish artist. I realized that what I was learning was so profound, I wanted to be sure to review my notes over and over again and share these Torah secrets with others. I began to write my notes in calligraphy. I had classical training and was already a professional calligrapher, and I began to "doodle." I knew that people would enjoy coloring in my doodles as they read and absorbed the wisdom on each page.

It really bothers me that, just like me at the beginning of my spiritual quest, so many Jewish people have no clue about the vast treasures of their own unique spiritual inheritance. It is urgent that we each do everything we can to understand how to prepare ourselves and the world for the great time of peace and abundance we have all been waiting for. In this time of violence and suffering and economic uncertainty, we each MUST do our utmost to bring Moshiach* (our long-awaited Redeemer) NOW!

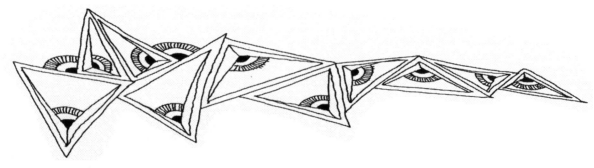

6

* See pages 10-11 for more information about Moshiach.

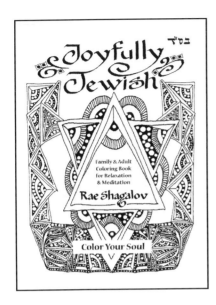

The *Joyfully Jewish* series began with the *Joyfully Jewish Family and Adult Coloring Book* that integrates the relaxing, meditative art of coloring with deep Chassidic secrets of Judaism.

It includes fun designs to color and unique Jewish quotes from contemporary Jewish masters written in beautiful calligraphy. It's an uplifting introduction to Jewish spirituality. The graphic images from that coloring book came from my Artnotes sketchbooks.

Create Your Joyfully Jewish Life is the first volume in the new *Joyfully Jewish* series of Artnotes. It includes many full-page and smaller images to color, but unlike the coloring book, it is much richer and fuller in calligraphy text and field notes. Most of the pages are copies of the original Artnotes pages, just as I wrote and drew them as I listened to the Torah classes.

But I don't want this book to be all work and no play.

Nor should it be only another passive, intellectual learning opportunity. I want this to be pleasant, interactive fun as well. It's very important for you to engage and interact with what you're learning so that you can really integrate it into your life in a joyful way. There are many places for you to color and record your thoughts, insights, good resolutions, doodles and dreams for your life and Geulah, the Messianic Era soon to come, please G-d.

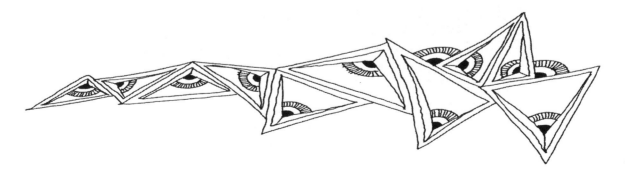

Suggested Supplies:

1. Paper
2. Notecards
3. Pens
4. Colored Pencils
5. Paper Plates
6. Sticky Notes
7. A Journal
8. Your favorite art supplies

I've also included Soul Adventures to help you integrate the profound Jewish wisdom you'll be learning in this book.

What is a Soul Adventure?

A Soul Adventure is a journey above time and space to explore the vast, fascinating chambers of your own soul and the G-dly hints, echoes, whispers, and holy sparks that are hidden in your innermost self.

Soul Adventures are creative exercises that help you look deeply at your life and make significant, transformative changes to improve it. Some of the Soul Adventures in this book were developed in *Joyfully Jewish* workshops that I have led. You can find more information about these workshops and author book-tours at the back of this book.

I WOULD LOVE TO SEE YOUR COLORFUL CREATIONS. Feel free to email me with questions, suggestions, personal insights or reflections you'd like to share – and, of course, I would love to see pictures of your coloring. Please share them with me via email at: info@holysparks.com or on any of my social media channels listed at the back of this book.

It is with great humility that I offer to you the first volume of Artnotes in my *Joyfully Jewish* series. It is my great hope that they will inspire you, deepen your love of Torah, increase your motivation to do mitzvahs, and help you feel closer to G-d every moment of your life.

May G-d bless the works of your hands with success, in good health, with great joy and abundant livelihood – and may you always be *Joyfully Jewish!*

May you be blessed with success and only good things!

Rae Shagalov

Holy Sparks

HOW TO USE THIS BOOK

SURROUND YOURSELF WITH INSPIRATION, ART & FRIENDS

Invite your family and friends to join you in the fun. The best way to be successful is to do the Soul Adventures with a friend to help you stay accountable to your personal growth.

This workbook is not intended to be read from beginning to end in one sitting. For best results, do them in order, but you can also skip around to what attracts you the most or spend a longer time with a Soul Adventure that you want to explore more deeply.

You can simply enjoy the calligraphy Artnotes and let the deep Jewish wisdom seep in and inspire you, or you can playfully interact with the wisdom by coloring in the images, writing and doodling on the journal pages, and engaging in the Soul Adventures. Some people use this book on their birthdays as inspiration for personal growth for the year.

Doodle

Explore your inner world through the prompts that are provided in each Soul Adventure. Sketch and twirl your pen in between writing your thoughts or if you feel stuck and unable to write. These doodles will relax and focus you and may provide a wealth of understanding of the subconscious and sublime whispers of your soul.

COLOR IT IN!

Coloring is a very relaxing, peaceful, meditative activity. As you color in the pages, contemplate the Artnotes thoughts on them, and try to internalize them. If you're doing this as a family activity, discuss the ideas while you color them in together. Afterwards, hang up your creations around your home to set a Joyfully Jewish tone to inspire you every day.

For best results, turn off the phone, computer and any other stressful distractions. Place a piece of cardboard or a few sheets of paper under the page if you are using pens so the ink won't bleed through. Intuitively choose your colors, and don't fret if you make a "mistake" or color outside the lines.

בס"ד

Living with Moshiach means going beyond your limitations.

IN THE TIME OF GEULAH, THE THINGS THAT LIMIT US NOW WILL NO LONGER BE LIMITATIONS. IF WE IMAGINE THAT WE ARE NOW IN THE TIME OF REDEMPTION, WHAT THAT LOOKS LIKE, FEELS LIKE, AND THEN ACT AS IF WE NO LONGER HAVE THOSE LIMITATIONS, THEN WE ARE LIVING WITH MOSHIACH.

The coming of Moshiach is a process. The world is gradually preparing itself for complete Truth.

We are engaging the entire world in G☐dliness.

WE HAVE BEEN SCATTERED ALL OVER THE WORLD, DOING MITZVAHS, ELEVATING EVERY BIT OF CREATION, IN ORDER TO STRENGTHEN AND PREPARE IT TO RECEIVE COMPLETE, UNRESTRAINED G☐DLINESS.

Holy Sparks
WWW.HOLYSPARKS.COM
© 2017 Rae Shagalov

When we do mitzvahs, we strengthen ourselves to be able to receive a greater level of light. In the time of Moshiach, there will be a tremendous revelation of G☐dliness. By doing Torah and mitzvahs, we will be ready.

UNEDITED NOTES   TEACHER UNKNOWN

I love to learn the secrets of Torah, about the intricacies of our soul, and how the universe is designed to help us transform this world into a dwelling place for G-d. With the help of G-d, over the last 25 years, I've gone to thousands of classes and written more than 3,000 pages of calligraphy Artnotes that give over the essence of each class.

This Jewish wisdom from hundreds of our greatest Torah scholars and teachers gives us a very important message for this special time at the threshold of the Messianic Era of peace, called the *Geulah*. I call these Artnotes the "field notes" of the last generation of exile and the first generation of Geula (the time of redemption & revelation of G-dliness).

When we do a mitzvah, we open the finite container of the object that we use and the space in which we do the mitzvah. MITZVAH BY MITZVAH, OBJECT BY OBJECT, INCH BY INCH, WE OPEN THE FINITE CONTAINERS OF EVERYTHING IN THIS WORLD, AND FILL EACH CONTAINER WITH THE INFINITE LIGHT OF G-DLINESS. WE ARE PREPARING THIS WORLD, OBJECT BY OBJECT, INCH BY INCH, FOR THE COMPLETE AND TOTAL REVELATION OF G-DLINESS. BY STRENGTHENING EACH THING THROUGH THE MITZVAHS THAT WE DO, WE ARE MAKING THIS WORLD READY TO RECEIVE THE ESSENCE OF G-D, FULL-STRENGTH, WITHOUT ANY HOLDING BACK. WHEN WE HAVE PREPARED EVERY LAST BIT OF THIS WORLD; WHEN WE HAVE ELEVATED EVERY OBJECT AND THE VERY LAST INCH OF SPACE ~ then... **Moshiach is here.**

The Lubavitcher Rebbe, Rabbi Menachem Mendel Schneerson, taught us that we must -- now -- "live with the Redemption," experience a foretaste of it and anticipate it in our daily conduct. This means living our lives in a way that parallels the way we would live in the time of the Redemption.

Moshiach & the Messianic Era: Moshiach is the Jewish messiah, the long-awaited Redeemer who will bring us out of the exile of this world into an amazing world filled with the revelation of G-dliness in every aspect of Creation. The word *Moshiach* in Hebrew means "anointed".

One of the principles of Jewish faith according to Maimonides is that one day there will arise a dynamic Jewish leader (Moshiach), who will be a direct descendant of the Davidic dynasty. He will gather the Jews from all over the world and bring them back to the Land of Israel, where he will rebuild the Holy Temple in Jerusalem.

In every generation, Moshiach is ready to be revealed when we have finished preparing the world to receive him. Every man, woman and child has an individual responsibility and priviledge to work to bring about Moshiach's coming, using his or her unique talents and situation.

11

Since the beginning of Creation and throughout all time, no one was created like YOU!

The soul descends to this world on a heroic journey to create a home for G-d.

Just as a puzzle is incomplete if one piece is missing – even if the puzzle has a million pieces – G-d created YOU because G-d needs you in this world.

Everyone was created to do a specific goodness or bring G-dliness to this world and to uniquely express G-d's infinite nature in our finite world. Everyone is essential. Every person has a part to play that only he or she can do, and the world will not be complete without that part – YOUR part!

So, what is it about you that made G-d create the uniqueness that is YOU?

What is your part in the Divine Plan?

Collectively, we all share a common purpose. What is that purpose? To bring holiness into the world with every step we take and every choice we make, in order to make this world into a comfortable, light-filled dwelling place for G-d.

But life is so complicated and confusing! How do we know what is our own individual contribution, and once we know it, how do we stay focused on it when we have so many desires, obstacles and distractions?

This workbook will help you:

- discover your absolutely unique purpose for being in this world

- guide you, step-by-step, in creating a clear action plan to achieve your goals successfully and joyfully without being overwhelmed

- get clear and stay focused on your goals and the things you value most in life

- help you envision your ideal life and the steps you can take to move forward into it.

There is no wrong way to answer the questions in this workbook. You don't have to answer every question. You don't have to fill out every page or do them in order. You can do a little if you don't have time to do a lot. Every bit of effort moves you forward. Do whatever works best for you!

The intent of this 30 day program is to help you to awaken your passionate vision and to encourage you to look deeply inside yourself to find the answers that lie within you. You'll find all of the tools you need to energize yourself with your joyful vision so that you can live a meaningful and happy Jewish life while you nurture your family and light up the world!

This workbook is designed as a 30 day program for break-through success, but guess what! Your success has already begun because you have decided you want to succeed. What's the proof? You're reading this right now.

Create Your Joyfully Jewish Life

Week One

☀ DREAMS OF FINE GOLD ☀

IN WHICH YOU WILL GET CLEAR ABOUT WHO YOU WANT TO BE

ב"ה

Take a deep breath...

Breathe G‑d in

Breathe
out...
        Negativity
        Anxiety
        Pain
        Fear
        Overwhelm

Just as you rely on G‑d for your next breath,
Rely on G‑d to carry you through everything!

Holy
Sparks
WWW.HOLYSPARKS.COM
© 2017 Rae Shagalov

Can you spare just one minute of your busy day to have a deep, relaxing moment with G-d? This is a meditation you can use anywhere, anytime, to reset yourself and your connection to G-d, strengthen your faith and feel peace in your heart. I call it, "The One Minute Miracle Meditation," because when you practice it, you can change your mood and your attitude in just a few breaths - in less than a minute!

16

The One Minute Miracle Meditation

Do This Meditation Before Each Soul Adventure

When we inhale, we are going to use our imagination to connect to our essence, our soul where it is connected to G-d.

As we breathe in, we are going to imagine that we are receiving our Breath of Life, joyfully and directly from G-d.

When we exhale, we are going to imagine that we are releasing everything that we don't want or need, everything that separates us from G-d — all of our negativity, fear, and anxiety.

1. Sit comfortably and take a moment to experience your breath. Just breathe normally and notice it.

2. Now, take a deep breath through your nose and let it out slowly. Fill your lungs with fresh, pure air and let it out slowly, releasing all of the toxins.

3. Do this a few times and notice how your body begins to relax.

4. Now, breathe deeply and connect to your innermost-self in the core of your being.

5. As you inhale, imagine that you are receiving your breath of air directly from G-d breathing into you. Feel the joy of that connection to G-d.

6. As you exhale, imagine that you are releasing every form of negativity from you.

Release everything that does not feel good — illness, pain, anxiety, fear.

Release every form of negativity. Just let it go when you breathe out.

That's it. It's that simple to remember who you are in your essence and to re-establish your connection to G-d in any moment. Just use your breath. In the space of a single breath you can change your attitude and your life.

Today, whenever any form of negativity arises, if you feel tired, irritable, angry, frustrated, or overwhelmed... Breathe out the negativity and breathe in G-d.

You can sign up for a free audio of "The One Minute Miracle Meditation at www.joyfullyjewish.com

בס״ד

What ties us together and keeps us together is chesed, loving-kindness.

Value every person for who he or she is.

APPRECIATE THE UNIQUENESS OF EVERYONE!

what God needs from us is to help those in need.

Kindness is the true nature of the world.

We change reality by helping one person, one household at a time.

IF EVEN ONE OTHER PERSON IN THE WORLD IS SUFFERING, I AM ALSO SUFFERING.

Take every opportunity to give and to grow.

Understand ◆ Sympathize ◆ Pray for another.

Being made in God's image means we were created to do good for no reason.

We are given free will in order to choose to use our free will to do acts of kindness.

The Test of whether or not we are doing an act of kindness with a Godly motive is: Is the Ego involved?

YOU KNOW YOU'VE DONE IT RIGHT WHEN IT LEADS TO ANOTHER MITZVAH, ANOTHER ACT OF KINDNESS.

Tisha B'Av 5764 OU "Be Good for Nothing"

UNEDITED NOTES

Holy Sparks
www.holysparks.com
© 2017 Rae Shagalov

⚡ STRETCH YOUR KINDNESS MUSCLES ⚡

בס"ד

A day shouldn't go by that you haven't done a kindness for someone! KEEP A NOTEBOOK AND RECORD IN IT THE KINDNESSES YOU DO EVERY DAY, AND THE KINDNESSES YOU INTEND TO DO THIS WEEK.

❧ Every act of kindness leads us step-by-step to G-d.* ☙

G-d created the world with kindness and we maintain the world with our acts of goodness and kindness. How? By being sensitive to the needs of others. Which others? First our family, friends and co-workers, then whoever we are divinely guided to meet in our day.

In relationships, small things are the big things: a greeting, a smile, an encouraging word - this is how we show our love for G-d's world. Compliments are free and do so much good in the world.

So, today, for our first Soul Adventure, we're going to consciously choose to do a small act of lovingkindness and see it as the true Soul Adventure that it is. Keep your eyes and ears open today for an opportunity to do chesed. Put a sticky note on this page to describe what you chose to do and how you or the other person felt about it. Repeat as often as you can.

May your next smile be the power that reverses the exile and brings Moshiach! ◆◇

*Rabbi Jonathan Rietti

EVERY PERSON HAS A כ KINDNESS IN HIS HEART

This kindness is a gift from Hashem.

Holy Sparks
www.HOLYSPARKS.COM
© 2017 Rae Shagalov

20

IN THE MOMENT OF CRISIS, YOUR ESSENCE COMES OUT.

DO ONE KINDNESS EVERY DAY.

START WITH YOUR FAMILY.

TRAIN YOURSELF TO BE A GIVER! THE MORE WE GIVE, THE HAPPIER WE ARE. חסד

Every morning, wake up and say: How can I give? To whom can I give?

KINDNESS IS THE MOTHERLODE OF BLESSING.

Just as our bodies need to eat, our souls need to give!

Are you giving with a whole heart?

IS YOUR KINDNESS TRULY LOVING AND PURE? OR ARE YOU SECRETLY EXPECTING SOMETHING IN RETURN?

IS YOUR GIVING SELFLESS? G‑D GIVES AND ALSO DOESN'T RECEIVE ANYTHING IN RETURN.

THINK: WHAT CAN I DO FOR THIS PERSON?

אהבת חסד

Is your Kindness truly Kindness?

Duct tape will not save us. So what will protect us?

חסד

Kindness

THE GIVER RECEIVES MORE FROM THE ONE WHO IS IN NEED, THAN THE NEEDY RECEIVES FROM THE GIVER.

"In the shadow of My palm I have covered you and I have protected you."

GIVING IS PRECIOUS TO OUR SOULS!

It is not enough to do Kindness

ANYONE WHO LEARNS TORAH AND PRACTICES KINDNESS CAN EXPECT DIVINE PROTECTION.
– CHAFETZ CHAIM –

WE NEVER LOSE BY GIVING!

EVERY ONE CAN BE A GIVER.

A GIVER IS CALM.

We have to want to do it. We have to love to do it. We have to run to do it!

The hallmark of our nation is Kindness!

GIVING IS WHY G‑D PUT US ON THIS EARTH. THIS IS HOW WE PERFECT OURSELVES. THIS IS HOW WE BECOME LIKE G‑D.

Chesed is a golden opportunity!

MAKE IT YOUR PASSION!

Giving is how we come close to G‑d.

PRETEND TO BE A GIVER UNTIL YOU REALLY ARE!

BEWARE! Run to do it! RESENTMENT NULLIFIES OUR KINDNESS. KINDNESS GREASES THE WHEELS OF HEAVEN.

GIVING IS A LIFE'S WORK. WE COME INTO THIS WORLD AS BABIES, THE ULTIMATE TAKERS. THROUGHOUT OUR LIFETIME WE LEARN TO GIVE.

Our Kindness to each other will bring us out of exile! 17.91

UNEDITED NOTES   TEACHER UNKNOWN

Bitachon is the absolute knowing, without any doubt, that G-d will make things good. The super power of bitachon is that your absolute trust in the lovingkindness of G-d increases your merit and becomes the conduit which draws down G-d's blessings to transform your situation for good.

ב"ה

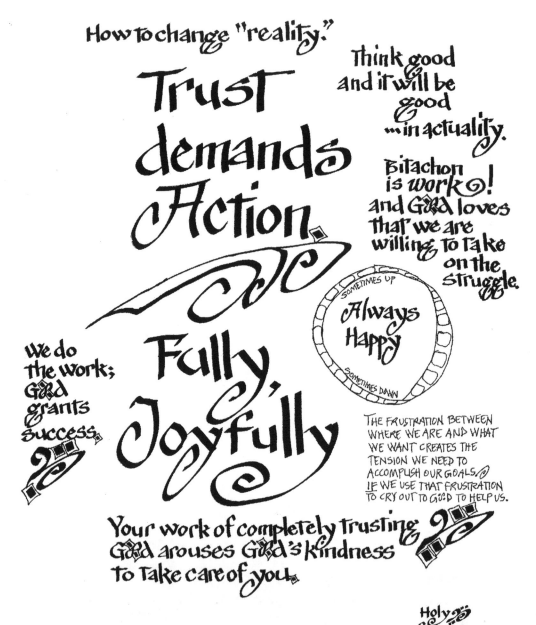

How to change "reality."

Trust demands Action.

Think good and it will be good ...in actuality.

Bitachon is work ☺! and G-d loves that we are willing to take on the struggle.

We do the work; G-d grants success.

Fully, Joyfully

SOMETIMES UP
Always Happy
SOMETIMES DOWN

THE FRUSTRATION BETWEEN WHERE WE ARE AND WHAT WE WANT CREATES THE TENSION WE NEED TO ACCOMPLISH OUR GOALS. IF WE USE THAT FRUSTRATION TO CRY OUT TO G-D TO HELP US.

Your work of completely trusting G-d arouses G-d's kindness to take care of you.

Holy Sparks

Shevat Farbrengen BAIS CHANA OF CALIFORNIA 5769

SOUL ADVENTURE ❖ DAY 3 ❖ (5 MINUTES)
☀ GROW YOUR TRUST IN G-D ☀

Trust produces a calm knowing that everything is for the good and everything will work out in the end. If G-d wants something to happen to you, nothing can stop it from happening to you. If it is not the will of G-d, then no one can cause you any harm. When we remember that everything happens precisely according to the Divine Will and that G-d loves us, it is easy to remain calm and alert, ready to recognize and receive our blessings.

Close your eyes and feel what it would be like to have total trust in G-d, to feel completely nurtured, protected, and safe, to know that absolutely everything in your life is ultimately for your good. Feel the excitement and passion of being G-d's partner in this world, as G-d trusts you to fulfill your part in co-creating the world with Him.

In an Ideal World, In Your Heart of Hearts...

If nothing stood in your way...
if you had the means to do whatever you wanted to do...
If you knew you would be successful...
if you had no worries, obstacles, obligations or limitations...
if you could be the kind of person you really want to be and do what you want to do most in this world -- what would you do?

Make a list of the things you would do today if you totally trusted in G-d.

By actively trusting in G‑d, we change our situation. ב"ה

Our trust arouses G‑d's mercy.

"*Tracht gut vet sein gut Think good and it will be good."

We are transforming concealed good into revealed good in our thoughts.

BY TRUSTING IN G‑D THAT G‑D IS GOOD AND THAT ALL WE RECEIVE FROM G‑D IS GOOD,

The awakening below will arouse an awakening above.

we transform ourselves.

A person who shows that he relies completely on G‑d arouses G‑d's mercy to provide for him.

G‑d is relying on you to make your unique contribution. That is why He created you. So you can rely on G‑d that you will be successful.

Connect to the Creator Who is All Good and wants only our good.

Transform the negative reality into a clear, positive vision.

Experience that vision emotionally as if it were happening right now.

Act to prepare for the revealed good, even while it is still concealed.

Holy Sparks
WWW.HOLYSPARKS.COM
© 2017 Rae Shagalov

Rabbi Y.Y. Shagalov & Rae Shagalov "Think good and It Will Be G‑d."

20.83

*The third Chabad Rebbe, the Tzemach Tzedek

ב"ה

Believing with my
whole heart:
God gives me everything
I need.

Faith
is
becoming
aware
of life,

R. SHLOMO HOLLAND

Looking at every
breath of life,
every blade of grass,
every star, every
grain of sand,
everything in your life.

Everything
is a
gift
from
God!

is
from
God!

Holy
Sparks

Tisha B'Av 5762

⟡ REMEMBERING YOUR ORIGINAL PURPOSE ⟡

G-d created each one of us with a unique purpose. We are in this world to fulfill the purpose that our soul was given before we came. Today, you will examine your purpose from above by imagining your soul's conversation with your Creator before you came to this world.

1. Take a deep breath and do the **One Minute Miracle Meditation.**

2. Exhale and release all negativity.

3. Now, picture yourself as the pure soul you were before coming into this world. Imagine that G-d is asking you to descend to this difficult world to be a partner in refining this world and doing a special job.

⟡ What do you think G-d asked you to do before you descended to this lower world?

⟡ What do you wish it was? You can totally make it up!

⊙ Write or Doodle Your Thoughts Below or in Your Journal. ⊙

If G‑d gave you a gift, you are obligated to use it and develop it for the Jewish people.

IF YOU HAVE A UNIQUE TALENT AND PURPOSE, WHAT IS IT? HOW CAN YOU DEVELOP IT?

We are all part of each other, each with our own unique purpose ◆

MOSES WAS בע"ה THE MOST HUMBLE MAN WHO EVER LIVED. WHY? HE KNEW...

Being humble

DOES NOT MEAN YOU SHOULD DENY THAT YOU HAVE ANY UNIQUE GIFTS OR TALENTS. BEING HUMBLE MEANS THAT YOU APPRECIATE THE UNIQUE GIFTS AND TALENTS OF OTHERS THAT YOU DON'T HAVE.

You should love your neighbor as yourself, but first...

YOU HAVE TO LOVE YOURSELF.

OUR SUCCESS IS THROUGH OUR INDIVIDUALITY.

G‑d Knows what is in the heart of every person.

THE SECRET OF SUCCESS AS A JEW IS TAKING WHATEVER IS NATURALLY EASY FOR YOU IN YOUR CHARACTER AND DEVELOPING IT FURTHER. EVERY JEW FEELS A CERTAIN CONNECTION TO SOME ASPECT OF BEING JEWISH @ CHESED, KINDNESS, PRAYER, HELPING OTHERS, VISITING THE SICK, TREATING GUESTS WELL, ETC. GROW INTO WHO YOU ALREADY ARE. MAKE THAT MITZVAH SHINE!

No one can do what you can do!

YEHUDA HAD THE QUALITY OF KINGSHIP. WHY? HE ADMITTED THE SOURCE OF HIS GREATNESS.

Gratitude

Start with your best character trait and polish it, refine it, improve it.

DEVELOP WHO AND WHAT YOU ARE!

WE LIVE IN A TIME WHEN UNIQUENESS AND INDIVIDUALITY IS NOT VERY WELCOME. DON'T GIVE UP WHO AND WHAT YOU ARE. WE NEED YOU!

THERE NEVER HAS BEEN AND NEVER WILL BE A JEW LIKE YOU!

Rabbi Y.Y. Rubinstein

"GETTING TO KNOW YOU" סוה I 5763 UNEDITED NOTES

 Holy Sparks

JEWISH LEARNING EXCHANGE

17.49

בס"ד

What a beautiful thing it is to be a Jew; what an honor!

Every soul is sent to accomplish its mission in this world.

① FOR WHAT ARE YOU NEEDED IN THIS WORLD?
② WHAT ARE YOUR TALENTS?
③ HOW CAN YOU USE YOUR TALENTS TO SERVE G‑D?

THE MORE LOVE YOU GIVE, THE MORE YOU BECOME ONE.

To love is...

To Give.

We are made in G‑d's image.

THE ULTIMATE SELF-PORTRAIT.

ARTISTS TRAIN THEIR EYES TO SEE FORM, BEAUTY, LIGHT IN THIS WORLD. JEWS TRAIN THEIR EYES TO SEE G‑D IN THIS WORLD.

TO BECOME ONE WITH G‑D WE GIVE.

אחד one

From the beginning of Creation and throughout all time, There is only one soul like you!

EMPTY YOURSELF OF SELF!

HOW? THROUGH A GREAT BIG SIGH.

FOR RABBI ENGEL'S MAGICAL MYSTERY TOUR

19.80

The mitzvah is the ultimate Jewish art form.

THE MITZVAH IS FILLED WITH THE PRESENCE OF G‑D.

DOING THE MITZVAHS IS GIVING TO G‑D WHAT G‑D WANTS TO RECEIVE FROM US.

THE BEGINNING POINT OF CREATION IS IN THE WHITE SPACE.

Jewish art is an expression of our heart.

TRANSFERRING CONSCIOUSNESS THROUGH THE HEART.

Hidur Mitzvah

BEAUTIFYING A MITZVAH.

613 Jewish talents

Begin from the Source

THERE IS NOTHING OTHER THAN G‑D!

THE INITIAL CREATION COMES FROM A MOMENT OF PURE NOTHINGNESS. FROM THIS TRUE NOTHINGNESS COMES THE ABILITY TO DRAW OUT A TRUE SOMETHINGNESS.

I AM RESPONSIBLE FOR BRINGING **THIS** OUT OF MY SOUL AND IF I DON'T, SOMETHING VERY IMPORTANT IS MISSING FROM THE WHOLE OF CREATION.

Suffering

IS INTENDED TO RE-ROUTE A PERSON WHO HAS GOTTEN LOST FROM HIS PURPOSE.

Holy Sparks

☀ LOOKING BACKWARD AT YOUR FUTURE LIFE ☀

⤙ The End is Embedded in the Beginning ⤚

Do you know how important you are to G☆d? G☆d needs you in this world to do what only you can do. So, what is it that you're here to do?

YOU are really REALLY SPECIAL! Yes, You!

Holy Sparks
www.HOLYSPARKS.com
© 2017 Rae Shagalov

Today, you will examine your purpose by working backwards through time, as if you were looking back at your life from sometime in the future.

Suppose you had your life to live over, only this time you were completely focused on your purpose. Imagine that Moshiach, the long-awaited Redeemer, is here and the world has been transformed completely into a world of good.

You have devoted your life to fulfilling your purpose, and you were successful and complete. You have achieved everything you ever wanted in life. You did exactly what you always longed for.

Work backwards through time. Start with the things for which you were most well-known, either publicly or just among your own family and friends. Include thoughts, words, deeds, your life's work and character traits.+

Read your vision of your ideal life to yourself
three times a day over the next four weeks
and watch how your life begins to change!

⇒ DREAMING UP YOUR IDEAL DAY ⇐

⇒ IMAGINE ⇐

Let go of your current reality. Go back up to the Throne of Glory, the home of souls, and get a new assignment — exactly the one you want. Then fly back down to this world and be born anew right now. This time you don't have to go through childhood. You can come right into adulthood (if you want to) and go straight to what you want to do and be in this world.

Write, draw, paint, collage or create symbols, music or a dance of what your life would be like if you were completely happy and satisfied with it. Write it out in detail, or find a partner who will write it for you while you describe your ideal life.

1. What are you doing from the time you wake up until the time you go to sleep?

2. What does your environment look like?

3. Who is the first person you greet? Who else is there with you throughout the day?

4. What are you feeling, smelling, eating, listening to, learning?

5. What are you wearing?

6. Where do you go?

7. What is happening in your spiritual and community life?

8. What are you doing for work? For fun?

Don't limit yourself to being practical. Let your imagination go wild. Pretend there are no obstacles at all. Write it in the present tense, as if it were already true. Use the next page or expand in your journal.

I am waking up in the morning and...

I feel...

I see...

I smell...

I hear...

This is what I do...

This is where I go...

This is whom I meet...

I am surrounded by...

בס"ד

Shabbos שבת

is the Soul of the world.
Shabbos gives us the power
to elevate time to Holiness.
Six days of the week we work
to separate the Holiness out of
the weekdays, doing good,
staying away from evil, sifting
the Holy Sparks that were hidden
in the week. Then everything
is elevated on
SHABBOS שבת

Shabbos is unchanging.
The weekdays are constantly
changing, up and down, up and down.
But on Shabbos, everything is complete.

❧ Envision the World-to-Come ❧

Save this Soul Adventure for the seventh day of the week which is the Jewish Sabbath, in Hebrew, Shabbat or Shabbos. Shabbos begins with the holy mitzvah of lighting candles 18 minutes before sundown on Friday, and ends when the first three stars come out, about 25 hours later, on Saturday night. Shabbos is a unique mini-journey for the Soul, a day of making time and space G-dly.

Shabbos is practice for the World-To-Come, weekly practice in living in a world that doesn't need fixing. What would you do in a perfect world? Shabbos is a time to feel as if all of the work of the previous week has been completed — that our lives and purpose have been fulfilled.

☉ ❧ A Note About Shabbos ❧ ☉

There are many laws pertaining to the Jewish people that prohibit us from doing certain kinds of work during the Sabbath, including writing. So, this adventure will take place in the mind and not on the page until after the Sabbath is over.

For more information about the amazing holiness of the Sabbath, and to get a free Shabbos Kit, go to: www.FridayLight.org

Imagine that the time of Redemption has arrived. Moshiach, the Redeemer for whom we have all been waiting, is here at last. The struggle is over. This is the first moment of Geulah, the era when all G-dliness is revealed, when every aspect of Creation - including all of us - has achieved its ultimate good.

There is nothing more to fix. We are not working on ourselves anymore. The work has all been done successfully. We now understand the purpose of our lives. The good that was hidden in every bad thing in the world since the beginning of time is now revealed. The world is fully at peace.

Imagine vividly what the world is like. Describe yourself, what you are like, what you are doing, who is with you, and what is happening around you. There are absolutely no limitations in this vision, except one. You have to have a physical body, but there are no limitations as to what that body can be and do. What was your part in bringing the World-to-Come?

Talk about it with your family and friends at the Shabbos table. Go over and over it again in your mind until your vision of Geulah and the World-To-Come is perfectly clear and easy to remember, because after Shabbos is over, you'll record it.

Melavah Malkah

Describe vividly what you envisioned over Shabbos -- the World-To-Come and your part in it. Record your vision in words, pictures, colors, collage or symbols, music, dance – whatever creative style suits you best. Describe in detail as above. Use additional pages and store them in your binder.

Melavah Malka means "Escorting the Queen." The evening after the Sabbath (Saturday night) is a special spiritual time for the soul to enjoy the lingering holiness of Shabbos and bring it into the week with encouraging words, stories of righteous people (especially the Baal Shem Tov), Torah thoughts and holy songs. It's also customary to have hot drinks (made with fresh water from the faucet) and delicious bread.

בס"ד

CANDLE LIGHTING BLESSING

בָּרוּךְ אַתָּה אֲדֹנָ-י אֱ-לֹהֵינוּ מֶלֶךְ
הָעוֹלָם אֲשֶׁר קִדְּשָׁנוּ בְּמִצְוֹתָיו
וְצִוָּנוּ לְהַדְלִיק נֵר שֶׁל שַׁבָּת קֹדֶשׁ

TRANSLITERATION:
BARUCH A-TA A-DO-NAY
ELO-HEI-NU ME-LECH HA-O-LAM
A-SHER KI-DI-SHA-NU
BI-MITZ-VO-TAV VI-TZI-VA-NOO
LI-HAD-LEEKNER SHEL SHA-BAT
KO-DESH.

TRANSLATION:
BLESSED ARE YOU, L-RD OUR G-D,
KING OF THE UNIVERSE, WHO HAS
SANCTIFIED US WITH HIS
COMMANDMENTS, AND
COMMANDED US TO KINDLE THE
LIGHT OF THE HOLY SHABBAT.

Lighting Shabbos
candles brings
peace, not only
to the family,
lighting Shabbos
candles illuminates
the whole world.

~ The Zohar ~

Sign up for more FREE art & coloring
pages at www.holysparks.com

This coloring page is from
The Joyfully Jewish Coloring Book
Available on Amazon.com

Holy Sparks ©1990-2016 **Rae Shagalov**

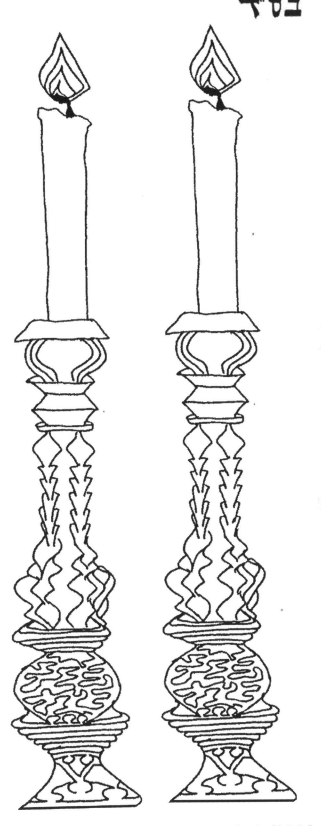

Enjoy coloring! But please do not color on Shabbat or other Jewish Holy Days.
The candle-lighting blessing printed here is sacred.
Please do not discard or desecrate

Torah is the inner essence of G‑d.

THROUGH THE TORAH, G&D IS TELLING US: "This is who I am. This is what I want. This is what I need." G&D HAS DECIDED TO NEED US, IN ORDER THAT HIS INFINITENESS CAN BE EXPRESSED EVEN IN THE FINITE.

Jews are in love with the Torah. We return to Torah again and again. Torah is our essence, our being, our lifeline. There is always a connection for every Jew to Torah. Torah is our channel of connection with G‑d.

How is it possible for us — tiny, little, finite creatures — to have a relationship with the Infinite Master of the Universe Who is beyond even the limitations of the infinite?

Truly we could never do it on our own. Only because G‑d, in His infinite kindness, gave us Torah and mitzvahs as a way to leap over from the finite to the infinite, can we achieve a relationship with Him.

G‑d gave us an opportunity to matter. Our purpose is to connect to G‑d's will and wisdom, to recognize and actualize the G‑dly view within the worldly view, and for the Divine to kiss the finite. Through our Torah and mitzvahs, we help build the inner structure of the world so that G‑d can dwell within it.

Torah is holy and refines us and teaches us why G‑d created us and what He expects from us. It's important for all of us to learn Torah and to love learning Torah, not just for the knowledge and information, but so that our soul can feel its intimate relationship with the Blessed Holy One.

Torah is G‑d's gift to us, a fascinating present to open every day. Look in the resources section for really wonderful, inspiring places to learn Torah.

בס"ד

The Torah is our roadmap

Holy Sparks

WWW.HOLYSPARKS.COM
© 2017 Rae Shagalov

RABBI MOSHE BRYSKI
RABBI SHAYA BERKOWITZ
UNEDITED NOTES

The Torah was given to us so that we could do the miraculous in a natural way, transforming dust to G☼dliness◇

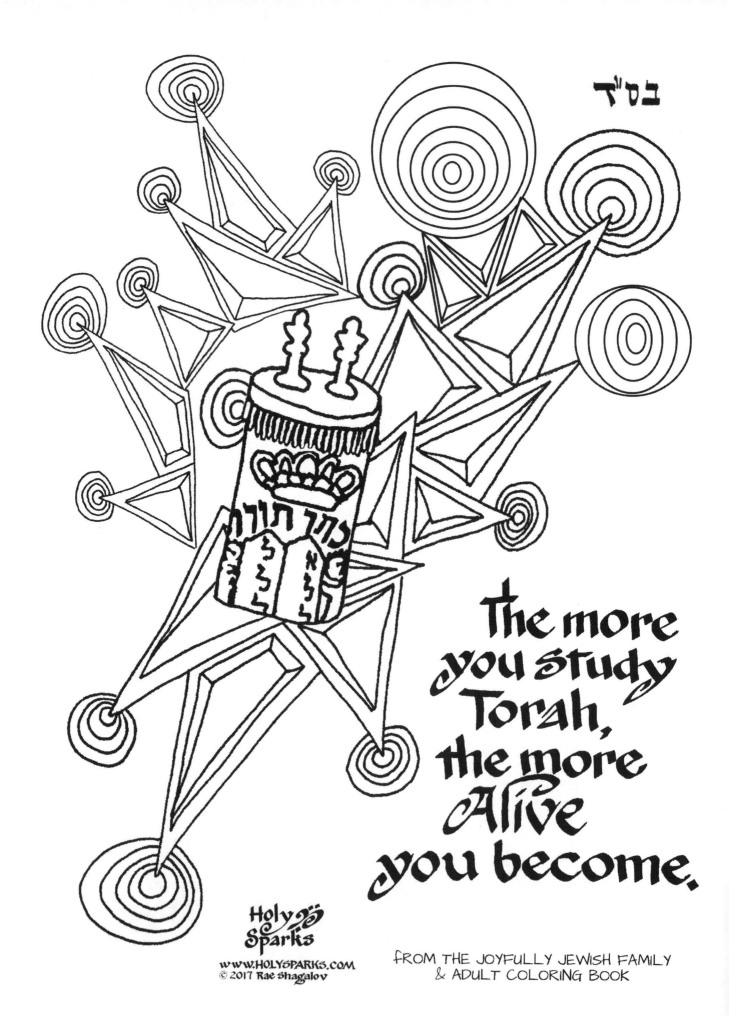

בס"ד

The more you study Torah, the more Alive you become.

Holy Sparks
www.HOLYSPARKS.com
© 2017 Rae Shagalov

FROM THE JOYFULLY JEWISH FAMILY
& ADULT COLORING BOOK

Every soul HAS A GARMENT OF TORAH AND A GARMENT OF MITZVAHS. THE MORE EFFORT YOU PUT INTO THE MITZVAH, THE MORE INTENT YOU PUT INTO THE TORAH YOU LEARN AND IN YOUR PRAYER, THE FINER YOUR GARMENT IN GAN EDEN. OUR BODIES COME AND GO, BUT OUR SOULS ARE FOREVER.

בס״ד

When you learn Torah you tap into the Divine Source of the world.

TORAH REACHES AN AREA OF THE WORLD THAT CANNOT BE TRANSFORMED BY ANY OTHER MITZVAH→ **your thought and your speech.** THIS IS WHY TORAH IS AS IMPORTANT AS ALL OF THE OTHER MITZVAHS TOGETHER.

Torah re-makes your Animal soul. YOUR ANIMAL SOUL DESIRES UNGODLY THINGS. IT IS UNAWARE OF ITS CREATOR. IT WANTS TO DO WHATEVER IT WANTS TO DO. YOUR G·dLY SOUL KNOWS ITS SOURCE. WHEN YOU STUDY TORAH, YOU ARE NOT ONLY DOING A G·dLY THING, YOU ARE CHANGING YOUR ANIMAL SOUL. YOU CANNOT CHANGE IT COMPLETELY, BUT YOU CAN MAKE YOUR MIND HOLY. IT DOES NOT ONLY CHANGE YOUR BEHAVIOR; IT CHANGES YOUR BEING, YOUR INNER SELF. TORAH CHANGES THE WORLD INSIDE YOU.

Torah reaches the inner condition of the human being and makes it HOLY.

Fill your heart with Torah

STUDY TORAH.
THE WORDS OF THE ALMIGHTY ARE INFUSED WITH HOLINESS. CHOOSE A LEARNED TORAH MENTOR. APPOINT A TIME TO LEARN EACH DAY. **Torah is spiritual food.** IT FEEDS OUR SOUL.

UNEDITED NOTES

Rabbi Reuven Wolf
Tanya

CREATE JOY

ב"ה

Holy Sparks
www.HOLYSPARKS.COM
© 2017 Rae Shagalov

Create Your Joyfully Jewish Life

Week Two

☀ PLANNING FOR SUCCESS ☀

IN WHICH YOU WILL GET CLEAR ABOUT WHAT YOU NEED TO DO

☀THE POWERFUL PAUSE ☀

You have two wills – and they are at WAR with one another. They are battling to rule the kingdom of YOU.

The good urge, or the *yetzer tov*, comes from the G-dly soul. The purpose of the *yetzer tov* is to bring more good into the world.

The Not-Good urge, or *yetzer hara* comes from the animal soul, and its purpose is to test you and bring out your inner powers by trying to stop the good from actualizing. The *yetzer hara* comes in many disguises. One of those disguises is "The Overwhelmster."*

The Overwhelmster's trick is to get us to hurry faster, faster, faster.

"Don't stop and think. Just **Do, Do, Do!!!!**

The first, most important thing to do when you're feeling overwhelmed is to do the complete opposite of what you might think:

☀PAUSE ☀

So, today's Soul Adventure is very simple.
You're going to **PAUSE** for 5 minutes.
Set a timer.
Pause.
Relax.
Release your hurry, your anxiety, your rush.
Take some long, slow, deep breaths.
Meditate.

⁓ **Connect** to **G-d** with **Joy** ⁓

Then ask yourself, "What am I doing here?"
Sit quietly until the answer comes.
And if no answer comes the first time you do this, don't worry.

You've still taken the time to re-connected to yourself and to G-d.

*You can learn more in depth how to defeat the Overwhelmster in the *Overcome Your Overwhelm* course at www.JoyfullyJewish.com

בס״ד

Running! Running! Running!
Running! Running! Running!

WHAT AM I DOING HERE?

SIT QUIETLY AND THE ANSWER WILL COME.

Holy Sparks
www.HOLYSPARKS.COM
© 2017 Rae Shagalov

SOUL ADVENTURE ❖ DAY 9 ❖ (5 MINUTES)
⋇ SELF-CARE -- CHECK IN WITH YOURSELF ⋇

You're going to take a 5 minute Powerful Pause again today and use the time to assess your energy and take care of yourself. So first...

⋇ PAUSE ⋇

The first step to overcome your overwhelm is to recognize what is going on. What are your personal signs when you are overwhelmed?

☐ Stress   ☐ Brain fog   ☐ Overtired or exhausted
☐ Fear   ☐ Tears   ☐ Too many projects
☐ Anger   ☐ Grief   ☐ Too much multi-tasking
☐ Irritability   ☐ Inner ache   ☐ Feeling of emptiness
☐ Back or Shoulder Pain   ☐ Shallow or fast breathing
☐ Any other pain   ☐ Tight feeling in your chest or throat
☐ Nagging doubts or worries   ☐ Things happening much too fast
☐ Feeling of falling or falling behind   ☐ Eating too much or the wrong things
☐ Weighed down by someone else's expectations of what you should be doing

☐ Other_____

Be gentle with yourself

Holy Sparks
WWW.HOLYSPARKS.COM
© 2017 Rae Shagalov

Take Care of Your Physical Needs

Often, when we're feeling overwhelmed, we forget about our physical needs, and that makes things even harder.

So, when you feel overwhelmed, check in with yourself.

- Are you thirsty or hungry?

  Eat & drink something that relaxes and energizes you.

- Too much sugar?

  Eat some protein, fat or whole grain.

- Not enough quality sleep?

  Take a power nap or meditate with deep breathing.

- Too much noise?

  Create a pocket of quiet time or solitude.

- Feeling empty, anxious, bored?

  Review your mission statement & strengthen your connection to G-d.

  [You'll learn how to craft your mission statement on Day 21.]

- Feeling depressed or stressed?

  Do something creative — Sing, dance, draw, write, smile.

- Body uncomfortable?

  Turn on some music and move & stretch in a way that you enjoy.

Listen to Your Body's Messages

What You'll Do

Bring a pen or some colored pencils and sit in a comfortable place.

1. Take a deep breath and let it out slo-o-o-o-wly.

2. Think about something in your life that you feel is very overwhelming right now.

3. Feel where in your body you are holding the stress of your overwhelm.

4. Sit for a moment and try to understand what your body is trying to tell you. What physical, emotional, or spiritual symptoms do you experience when you think of what feels overwhelming to you?

Simple Stress Relief

❧ Is that pain in your shoulders telling you that you're carrying too much on your shoulders?

✦ Roll your shoulders and imagine what might be falling off to relieve your burden.

❧ Is the ache in your lower back telling you that you're working too hard and don't feel supported?

✦ Is there someone you can ask to help you with one thing?

Make notes to remember where you're experiencing discomfort and what that part of your body might be expressing.

PAUSE

Relax and assess what's really going on with you so that you can start to make some good changes to unravel the overwhelm in your life.

בס"ד

What is your body Telling you?

בס"ד

YOU ARE WHERE YOUR MIND IS

The freedom of the mind comes through JOY

REBBE NACHMAN OF BRESLOV

Simply Tzfat   June 29, 5760

Holy Sparks

WWW.HOLYSPARKS.COM
© 2017 Rae Shagalov

ב"ה

10 Soul Tips To Reduce Stress & Pressure By Increasing Your Faith & Connection to G-d

① Recognize the signs of pressure, relax, and breathe light into them.

HEART ♥ ◆ HEAD ◆ THROAT ◆ NECK ◆ SHOULDERS ◆ BACK ◆ STOMACH ◆ LUNGS ◆ FAST HEART BEAT ◆ FAST, SHALLOW BREATHING ◆ HEAT IN FACE ◆ ?

② Create white space in your life, with your breath.. Breathe G-d In... Breathe Stress Out... Create an infinite moment with your breath.

③ Talk to G-d
◆ KVETCH ◆ COMPLAIN ◆ PRAISE ◆ THANK ◆ BEG
Ask for whatever you need. Create a loving relationship with the Master of the Universe.

④ Call up a friend and ask for a Blessing. Join your two souls together to create a bigger channel for the Blessing to come into.

⑤ BE NEW. Tap into the LIFE FLOW of CREATION in this moment right now!

⑥ Gam zu l'tova This, Too, is for the good!
HIDDEN IN EVEN THE DARKEST SITUATIONS (YOU SHOULD NEVER KNOW FROM THEM!) IS A **Holy Spark** OF GOOD FOR YOU TO FIND AND RETURN AS YOUR GIFT TO G-D. WHAT GOOD, WHAT INNER STRENGTH CAN YOU FIND IN YOUR SITUATION?

⑦ Tracht Gut ver Sein Gut Think Good and It Will Be Good!
FOCUS ON WHAT YOU WANT INSTEAD OF WHAT YOU DON'T WANT. LIVE IN YOUR VISION OF YOUR IDEAL LIFE AS IF IT WERE REAL @ AND IT WILL BECOME REAL IN WAYS YOU CAN'T EVEN IMAGINE.

⑧ Give charity. When you give, G-d gives. When you show kindness, G-d's blessing is drawn down into this world.

⑨ Prevent Pressure with a flexible plan that keeps you inspired and connected to G-d and focused on your purpose and priorities at a comfortable pace.

⑩ Gratitude Focus on the good you have, instead of on what you lack, and thank G-d for it.

Holy Sparks
WWW.HOLYSPARKS.COM
© 2017 Rae Shagalov

⇝Unpack the Cluttered Closet of Your Mind⇜

You know **THAT** closet.

The one that is stuffed with things you had to get out of the way in a hurry... or the Junk Drawer. Our minds get cluttered like that, too.

In this part of our Journey, we're going to do a Mind Flow and pour out all of the thoughts, needs, lists and worries that are cluttering up our minds so that our thinking will feel clear and spacious.

Then, we're going to reorganize all of those cluttered thoughts so that our priorities emerge and the rest can be saved for another time.

Most people have many different roles and responsibilities - family, work, hobbies, friendships, Torah study and mitzvahs. There's cooking and cleaning, exercising and staying in touch with extended family and friends, communal responsibilities

– and then there is Shabbos.

And all of the Jewish holidays.

So many holidays to prepare for our families and guests!

Yikes! How do we do it all?!!!

Well, there are To Do lists.

I don't know about you, but my To Do lists can get so long I'm exhausted just looking at them!

That's when I discovered that my To Do list was actually one of the tools used by the Yetzer Hara (that part of us that does **NOT** want us to be successful). Although it can definitely be helpful to write down what needs to be done, a long list is the **WORST** way to do it.

INTRODUCING THE MIND FLOW SYSTEM

⊙ No More Long, Intimidating Lists! ⊙

In this adventure, we're going to start unpacking the overwhelming To-Do's so we can create a spacious, relaxed, and productive mind. Once you write down a list, you only have two choices:

1. Get it done and cross it out, or

2. Leave it undone and perhaps add it to a new list.

The Mind Flow unpacking system is much more flexible.

You'll make a list, but each item will be on its own sticky note.

Then you can move the sticky notes around and prioritize them or sort them by categories. Instead of being overwhelmed by a long list, you'll tuck away those sticky notes into the proper place (you'll learn more about how to do that in tomorrow's adventure). Then your mind will be clear and spacious to give your attention to one priority at a time.

You will feel more settled and focused because your thoughts are now organized instead of a **tumble jumble** in your brain.

⊙ What You Will Need ⊙

You'll need two paper plates, a pen or pencil, and a pad of sticky notes for this adventure.

What You'll Do

1. On one plate, write: **VERY IMPORTANT**

2. On the 2nd plate, write: **CAN WAIT**

Now, write down everything you feel you need to do.

1. Write one item on a sticky note.

2. Intuitively sort the sticky notes onto the two plates.

3. Use as many sticky notes as you need to get everything out of your mind and onto a sticky note.

When your house circuits are overloaded, you search to find what can be unplugged or turned off to free up the circuits for what is essential.

That's what we're doing in this Soul Adventure.

Taking a few minutes to sort your priorities will clear up so much room in your mind that everything you need to do will flow much more easily. You'll have much greater clarity and concentration for the things you choose to do because you'll know they are most important to you.

Just this sorting (of very important/can wait) might be a good enough way to clear your mind for a focused, happy, and productive day. Over the next two days, we're going to drill down and get even more focused. We're going to choose one goal at a time and break it down further for even more clarity and for successful completion of our goals.

⚡ TOO MANY PRIORITIES? ⚡
Limit & Let Go!

↠ What if it's still too much?! ↞

Right now, I'm doing just this one thing.

Effort

WHATEVER WE CAN DO, WE DO. THE REST IS UP TO OUR PARTNER IN HEAVEN. **How much should I try?** IF I THINK I RUN THE SHOW, THERE IS NO LIMIT TO THE EFFORT I CAN MAKE. BUT WHEN I REMEMBER THAT THE MASTER OF THE UNIVERSE RUNS THE SHOW AND ACCOMPLISHES ALL THINGS, THEN I DO WHAT I CAN DO AND LEAVE THE REST TO HASHEM. **G‑d will help you but G‑d wants you to do your part**

Rebbetzin Leah Kohn
JEWISH LEARNING EXCHANGE/JEWISH RENAISSANCE CENTER
UNEDITED NOTES

What if you find that EVERYTHING feels like a priority?

Did you stack most of your sticky notes on "**Very Important**" plate? Most likely that means one of two things:

1. You are saying yes to more than you can handle.

2. You are afraid to let go of control.

Choose ONE thing to focus on and finish.

Put only that one sticky note on a new plate.

⚡ MEDITATE ⚡

RIGHT NOW, I AM DOING JUST THIS ONE THING.

WITH G‑D'S HELP, I WILL SUCCESSFULLY COMPLETE IT.

Now, go do that one thing with happy clarity.

May we be blessed to free ourselves from our limitations and utilize the potential of this day

Break it down into little easy pieces.

A Story:

A king once asked his son to do a job for him.

It was the first time the king asked his son to take responsibility for something important, so of course the prince wanted to do it well.

The king asked the prince to move a very large rock from one end of the kingdom to the other.

The prince directed many men and horses and cranes, but the rock was so large that all together they could not move the rock.

After one year the king returned and saw the boulder had not been moved.

The prince said, "The task was too hard for me."

The King said, "My son, I love you too much to waste your time by asking you to do something that is impossible for you. I do not expect you to move the whole rock at once. Break it up into small pieces and move it a little at a time."

This story is a parable. The most important part of us, our souls, are living in the palace of the King. The king has sent us away from the palace and asked us to move a very large rock –

Our ego.

So how do we do it? We break up our ego into small pieces. We improve our character traits a little bit at a time. This is also a great tip for managing any large or overhelming task.

58

Break Down Your Overwhelm Into Little Baby Steps

I have a confession to make.

After Shabbat, especially when we've had a table full of guests, I look at the mess and I just want to sing, "Tra lala lala... See you later!"

Then I find one thing on the table that I can easily put away.

"I'm just going to put this ONE little thing away," I say to myself, "And THAT'S ALL!!!!." And you know what? I see another little thing I can throw away... and then another thing it wouldn't be too hard to rinse... And before you know it, the messy table is clear.

I work on many projects, large and small, and the single most valuable technique I've ever learned to get things done is to break every job into smaller action steps.

How to Use the Baby Steps Tool

The Baby Steps Tool is the easiest way to "break the boulder up into little pieces." You can use sticky notes on it, write on it directly, copy it so you can use it again for the next project, or make a new one by drawing lines on a paper plate.

Now it's time to take one of those sticky notes from the "Unpack the Closet of Your Mind" adventure. Stick it on the Baby Steps Tool and break it down into smaller steps. What is your first or most important step? Which Baby Step seems the easiest, fastest, or most pleasant to do? Start with that one and with G-d's help the rest will flow.

ב"ה

Nurture your dream with teeny, tiny delightful baby steps.

Holy Sparks

www.HOLYSPARKS.COM
© 2017 Rae Shagalov

Write one step for each section. You don't have to fill out every section, but the smaller the steps you can make out of your big job, the faster and easier it will be to complete it pleasantly.

One or more of your baby steps might be extra challenging and need a Baby Step Tool of its own to break it down into smaller, easier-to-do pieces.

Do what you absolutely must, and take off your list what you can't do, or don't want to do (if it isn't an absolute necessity.) Try to delegate as much as you can.

Another Tip is to set a timer for just 5-20 minutes and commit to doing your Baby Steps until the timer goes off.

⊙⤴ USE COLOR! ⤴⊙

Of course, you can also color it with your markers, paints or pencils and use different colors for each Baby Step. That little bit of creativity will make it more delightful to use and review.

⤴ Know Your Overwhelm Set-Point ⤴

This will differ for everyone, of course. We all have different thresholds of tolerance for multi-tasking, stress, and pressure.

Know yours,

Recognize when you're getting close to it so that you can do these steps before you reach the point of melting down from overwhelm.

If you still feel resistance, don't worry. Keep doing the One Minute Miracle Meditation and breathe right through your resistance by connecting to G-d.

Just do what you have to do!
THIS IS A VERY HIGH LEVEL IN THE SERVICE OF G·d.
DO WHAT YOU HAVE TO DO AND G·d WILL SURELY HELP.

YOUR 4TH SPIRITUAL POWER TOOL
❋ BLESSING ❋

We have a blessing for almost everything! There are blessings for mitzvahs, food, water, rainbows, earthquakes, thunder, and many more.

Jewish tradition teaches us that we are supposed to say 100 formal blessings a day. While that might sound like a lot, most of them are built into our daily prayers. Plus there are blessings we say when we awaken, before and after we eat, after using the bathroom, before doing mitzvahs, and when we go to sleep.

Beyond the formal blessings, we also have a tradition to bless each other.

Every Jew has the ability to give blessings. NEVER UNDERESTIMATE THE POWER OF EVEN THE SIMPLEST JEW TO BRING BLESSING FROM ABOVE TO BELOW.

Chassidus teaches us that the word *bracha* (blessing) literally means "drawing down," from the word "braicha" (a channel). Every blessing in life needs to be drawn down from its potential, spiritual state into the actuality of our physical world.

It's all there—health, happiness, success, prosperity, wisdom, peace. Spiritually we are all healthy and happy, wealthy and wise. The obstacles we experience in life are a reflection of the constriction we are experiencing in our connection to G-d. One of the ways we can help each other open that constriction &connect to G-d is through blessing.

We all need blessings in our life. There is only so much that we can do on our own. We can visualize our ideal life, we can pray and ask G-d to provide what we need, we can set goals and take action to bring what we want into being, but without G-d's blessing, what we need will not descend. The good news is that everyone can bestow a blessing. Our sages say that if we knew our own power of blessing, we would never stop blessing each other! So how does it work?

בָּרוּך אַתָּה

WHEN YOU MAKE A BLESSING,
REMEMBER WHO THE YOU IS
THAT YOU ARE SAYING THE
BLESSING TO.

From the lowest
to the highest
to the lowest

By making
a blessing,
we draw G‑d
down into this world.

Rabbi Simcha Bart on Tefillah BAIS CHANA OF CALIFORNIA
UNEDITED NOTES

Holy Sparks
WWW.HOLYSPARKS.COM
© 2017 Rae Shagalov

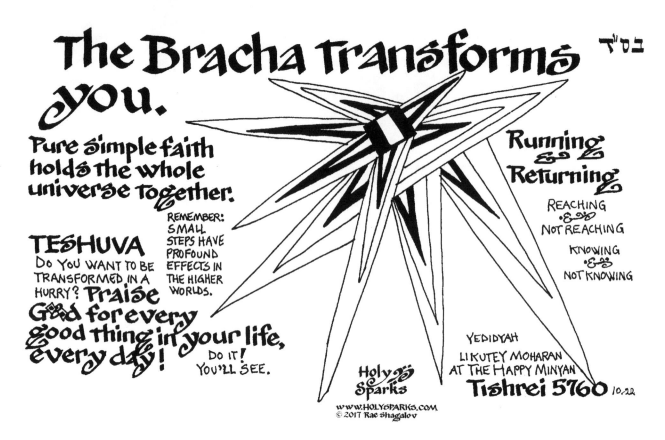

The Bracha Transforms you.

בס"ד

Pure simple faith holds the whole universe together.

REMEMBER: SMALL STEPS HAVE PROFOUND EFFECTS IN THE HIGHER WORLDS.

TESHUVA
DO YOU WANT TO BE TRANSFORMED IN A HURRY? **Praise God for every good thing in your life, every day!** DO IT! YOU'LL SEE.

Running & Returning

REACHING & NOT REACHING

KNOWING & NOT KNOWING

YEDIDYAH
LIKUTEY MOHARAN
AT THE HAPPY MINYAN
Tishrei 5760 10.22

Holy Sparks
WWW.HOLYSPARKS.COM
© 2017 Rae Shagalov

Perhaps your friend wants to get married, but she is having difficulty finding her soulmate. You feel compassion for her and you would like to help her, but you don't know of anyone for her. What can you do?

There is something very powerful you can do, and it only takes a moment. You can bless her. From the depths of your heart, you can say, "May G-d bless you to find your true soulmate, and may we all merit to dance at your wedding soon!"

Then, actually sing a little bit of a wedding tune and dance a few steps with her.

With your profound love for your friend, you have used your own connection to G-d to open wider the channel of blessing for your friend so that with G-d's help, her potential can be actualized in this world. You have danced a few steps with her past her limitations.

Your friend needs the blessing because she has reached the limit of her own spiritual resources. With your lovingkindness, you bond your spiritual self with your friend's spiritual self to make a new expanded self.

In this way, you broaden the channel of blessing so that your friend can move past her constriction and receive more of the resources of her own soul. What a great gift to give to your friend!

בס"ד

Words of Torah shared at the table.

Leave a little over for God. PUT A PORTION OF YOUR FOOD ASIDE ON YOUR PLATE TO TRAIN YOURSELF TO EAT A LITTLE LESS THAN YOU ARE USED TO.

A blessing. A PERSON WHO EATS WITHOUT MAKING A BLESSING IS LIKE ONE WHO STEALS FROM THE POWERFUL BENEVOLENCE OF THE ONE WHO PROVIDES FOR THE WORLD.

A good heart is a continuous feast. WHEN YOU APPRECIATE WHAT YOU HAVE & WHATEVER YOU HAVE IS A FEAST. @MISHLEI@

What makes eating holy?

Eating for the sake of Heaven.

To serve a higher level of holiness we eat food that is refined by the laws of kashrus.

The blessing sanctifies the food. THE BLESSING ACKNOWLEDGES THE SOURCE OF THE FOOD AND IMBUES THE FOOD WITH HOLINESS.

The after-blessing releases the holiness of the leftovers and thanks God for the food.

I'm eating to give me strength to serve God. THIS THOUGHT MAKES EVERY MEAL A SEUDAT MITZVAH.

Meditate for a minute before you eat: Where did your food come from? @R. AVIGDOR MILLER@ FROM SEED TO BREAD @ HOW MANY PEOPLE PARTICIPATED IN THE PROCESS OF MAKING THE FOOD THAT YOU ARE EATING? THANK GOD FOR THE TREMENDOUS EFFORT THAT WENT INTO THE BREAD YOU ARE EATING.

Holy Sparks
www.HOLYSPARKS.COM
© 2017 Rae Shagalov

UNEDITED NOTES   TEACHER UNKNOWN

☀ USE YOUR SUPER POWER OF BLESSING ☀

⊙ GIVE A BLESSING TO FAMILY & FRIENDS ⊙

For today's Soul Adventure, give someone a beautiful blessing.
It only takes a moment of your time – and it's free!

בס"ד

WRITE YOUR BLESSING HERE:

Holy Sparks
www.HOLYSPARKS.COM
© 2017 Rae Shagalov

ברכה בריכה

BREICHA IS A POOL. ASKING FOR SOMETHING NEW IS TEFILAH OR PRAYER. THERE IS A SPIRITUAL POOL AVAILABLE TO ALL OF US. THE TZADDIK CAN SEE INTO THAT POOL AND DRAW DOWN FROM IT TO US. THE TZADDIK CAN BE A CONDUIT THAT DRAWS FROM THE POOL OF BRACHAS AND BRING THEM INTO THIS WORLD EXPANDED & REVEALED. WHEN WE CALL HASHEM'S NAME WE DRAW G-D'S ENERGY TOWARD US.

בריח

A BOLT THAT DRAWS FROM ONE SIDE TO ANOTHER TO LOCK FIRMLY.

4 TYPES OF BLESSINGS

1. Blessings on mitzvahs
2. Blessings of Praise
3. Blessings of Thanksgiving
4. Blessings on Food

CONDUITS OF DIVINE ENERGY

Requesting our needs from the BLESSED ONE

LIKE A SERVANT ASKING FOR GIFTS FROM HIS MASTER.

PRAYER should BE A SILENT SCREAM — BAAL SHEM TOV

LIKE A PAUPER BEGGING AT THE DOOR.

IF YOU SEARCH YOU'LL FIND

IN EVERY PLACE WE FOUND G-D'S GREATNESS THERE WE FOUND G-D'S HUMILITY.

אמן

IT'S TRUE AND I BELIEVE THE BLESSINGS OF THE BLESSER

AND SO IT SHOULD BE. THE ALMIGHTY WILL BLESS AND FULFILL THE REQUESTS OF THE PRAYER.

THERE IS NO KING IN THIS WORLD WHO DOES NOT RECEIVE HIS INSTRUCTIONS FROM ABOVE.

אמן

EACH OF THE 70 NATIONS HAS AN INNER DIMENSION & A SPIRITUAL FORCE THAT GUIDES IT ACCORDING TO HASHEM. ISRAEL, HOWEVER, HAS NO INTERMEDIARY. THE ENERGY COMES STRAIGHT TO THE LAND OF ISRAEL DIRECTLY FROM HASHEM WITHOUT ANY PRECONDITIONS. FROM ISRAEL THE SUSTENANCE SPREADS OUT TO THE ENTIRE WORLD.

TRUE IS THE BLESSING THAT THE BLESSER BLESSED

WE CLIMB THE RUNGS OF THE LADDER OF PRAYER UNTIL WE GRAB THE ANGELS BY THE TOES.

NEXT YEAR AT THIS TIME MAY YOU BE A WEALTHY & LEARNED JEW

3.54 1996

ASCENT   Rabbi Shaul Leiter & CHAYA BRACHA Leiter   Holy Sparks

www.HOLYSPARKS.COM
© 2017 Rae Shagalov

UNEDITED NOTES

בס"ד

THE
BLESSING
descends
AND
IS
REVEALED
THROUGH
US

There are many kinds of barriers and limitations: There are those from within and those from without, barriers between people, barriers that prevent us from doing good things and the limitations of our own minds.

There are the barriers that exist simply because we are limited beings. There is one spiritual power tool that breaks though all limitations, and that is the power of joy.

The joy on Shabbos is incredible!

Holy Sparks
WWW.HOLYSPARKS.COM
© 2017 Rae Shagalov

⟫ Shabbat ⟪

⟫ The Joy Meditation ⟪

"Joy breaks through all barriers."

·⟫· Our Sages ·⟪·

Today, we will learn how to turn on the power of Joy in any moment.

1. Take a deep breath and let it out slowly, almost like a big sigh.

2. Close your eyes and remember an extremely joyful moment of your life.

3. Take a few moments and try to fully relive and experience the feelings you felt in all of their intensity at that exquisite moment of joy.

4. Once you are experiencing that joy vividly, bring it from memory into the present moment and open your eyes.

5. Use that past joy to inspire you today. Try to turn on this joy at random moments at least twice more today by remembering that joyful time and re-experiencing it.

Where there is joy, the Infinite Divine Presence, which has no limits, can enter and break through your limitations!

Remember that the same Divine Light that was in that joyful experience is in your life today. The joy you felt in that moment you can also feel today in any moment. Whenever you are experiencing a sense of anxiety, constriction, or lack in your life, do this brief meditation to shine the light of joy on the darkness of your situation. Use the power of joy as fuel to burst through your barrier.

☉⤙ On Shabbos After Candle Lighting.. ⤚☉

On Shabbos, after candlelighting, sit by the flames for a few minutes and re-experience your Joy Meditation. Shabbos is a joyful time with G-d.

From Shabbos, the whole week is blessed.

ON SHABBOS, MEDITATE ON WHAT BLESSINGS SHOULD COME FROM YOUR SHABBOS INTO YOUR WEEK.

Imagine again that the time of Redemption has arrived, and the whole world is filled with joy. Moshiach, the Redeemer for whom we have all been waiting, is here at last. There is no more pain or suffering. This is the first moment of Geulah, the era when all G-dliness is revealed, when the whole world is now surrounded by goodness and filled with kindness.

The joyful purpose that was hidden in every hurtful thing in the world since the beginning of time is now revealed. The world is fully at peace. Imagine vividly what this joyful world is like. Over Shabbos, ask your family and friends to share what makes them feel happy.

⤜❈ Melavah Malkah ❈⤛

☉⤙ After You See Three Stars in Three Different Parts of the Sky ⤚☉

Melavah Malka means "Escorting the Queen." The evening after the Sabbath (Saturday night) is a special spiritual time for the soul to enjoy the lingering holiness of Shabbos and bring it into the week with encouraging words, stories of righteous people (especially the Baal Shem Tov), Torah thoughts and holy songs. It's also customary to have hot drinks (made with fresh water from the faucet) and delicious bread.

After, Havdalah, the ritual for separating the Holy Sabbath from the rest of the week, record any insights you might have had over Shabbos.

⤜❈ Gather your family or friends together for a Melavah Malka Farbrengen (Gathering) with a focus of sharing joyful memories and stories. ❈⤛

As you share with each other encouraging words and stories, each person can mention what he or she needs for the coming week. Then you or anyone present can make a blessing to help your friend expand the resources of his or her soul and connect to G-d in preparation for receiving their blessings. Everyone else should answer with a heartfelt "Amen" to confirm the blessing. In this way everyone joins in to make an even more "expanded self" so that the channel of blessing is as wide as it can possibly be.

בס"ד

To make a little bit holier the rest of the week...
MELAVAH MALKAH

BE HAPPY WITH WHAT YOU HAVE

KEEP ON GOING! HOLD ON WITH JOY!

BE HAPPY WITH WHAT YOU ARE!

Make your song a praise to Hakodesh Baruch Hu. THERE ARE TIMES WHEN WE HAVE TO RUN AFTER OUR BELOVED. THERE ARE TIMES WHEN WE ARE SO FAR AWAY WE HAVE TO MAKE A GREAT EFFORT TO COME CLOSER TO OUR BELOVED. HOW PLEASED IS OUR BELOVED WHEN WE MAKE THAT SPECIAL EFFORT.

"JOY HEALS EVERYTHING

THE WHOLE YEAR HAPPY!

Happiness is LIFE

WHETHER WE ARE UP OR WHETHER WE ARE DOWN, THE IMPORTANT THING IS TO COME CLOSE TO HASHEM.

We have no idea how powerful are the blessings we give to one another. IF WE ONLY KNEW, WE WOULD NEVER STOP BLESSING EACH OTHER!

Happy Minyan Melavah Malkah, August 7 5759

WITH BRESLOVER CHASSIDIM FROM TZFAT
UNEDITED NOTES

Holy Sparks

www.HOLYSPARKS.COM
© 2017 Rae Shagalov

Please do not color on Shabbat or Yom Tov.

Jewish nature is to push, to go higher.

THERE IS NEVER A SITUATION IN LIFE IN WHICH G·D ABANDONS YOU.
① ACKNOWLEDGE THAT G·D PUT YOU IN YOUR SITUATION.
② IN EVERY SITUATION, NO MATTER HOW PAINFUL OR DIFFICULT, G·D TALKS TO YOU AND TELLS YOU WHAT HE EXPECTS YOU TO DO NOW.

ב"ה

WHEN WE STOOD AT MOUNT SINAI,

Every Jew recognized his letter in the Torah.

THE HOLIEST THING IN THE WORLD IS A SEFER TORAH, BUT IN ORDER FOR IT TO BE HOLY, IT HAS TO HAVE ALL 600,000 LETTERS.

EVERY LETTER IN THE TORAH HAS A POSITION IN WHICH IT MUST BE.

No letter in the Torah is more important than any other.

THE ע OF AMALEK IS JUST AS IMPORTANT AS THE מ OF MOSHE, BECAUSE WITHOUT IT, THE TORAH WOULD NOT BE HOLY.

There are 600,000 letters in the Torah. If it is missing even one letter, then the Torah is not Holy.

Everyone has an important mission in life.

IN THE POSITION IN WHICH YOU ARE, YOU ARE FULFILLING A GOAL WHICH NOBODY ELSE CAN FULFILL.

5764

Every soul is planted in the situation in which he is.

Everyone has his or her mission in life.

You have to understand who you are.

YOU HAVE TO UNDERSTAND WHAT YOU CONTRIBUTE AND COMPLETE IN THE JEWISH PEOPLE.

Every Jew has an important message that only he or she can deliver to the Jewish people by living his or her life to the fullest.

MOSHE RABBEINU WAS A VERY SIGNIFICANT SOUL IN THE JEWISH PEOPLE. WE MIGHT FEEL INSIGNIFICANT COMPARED TO MOSHE RABBEINU, BUT WITHOUT YOUR SOUL AND MY SOUL, THE JEWISH NATION WOULD NOT BE COMPLETE, IT WOULD NOT BE HOLY. WITHOUT YOUR SOUL AND MY SOUL, THERE WOULD BE NO MOSHE RABBEINU.

Your complaints, your limitations are your situation, your position in life.

THIS IS YOUR CUSTOMIZED POSITION IN THE JEWISH NATION THROUGHOUT TIME, IN WHICH G·D PLACED YOU SO THAT YOU WILL BE ABLE TO MAKE YOUR UNIQUE CONTRIBUTION TO THE JEWISH PEOPLE.

No matter what your situation is, G·d put you there.

UNEDITED NOTES   9HOD OF GEVURAH@

Rabbi Ezriel Tauber "The Courage to Rise Above"

TODAY IS 12 DAYS WHICH ARE ONE WEEK & FIVE DAYS OF THE OMER.

IN HONOR OF MY HUSBAND

Holy Sparks
WWW.HOLYSPARKS.COM
© 2017 Rae Shagalov

Create Your Joyfully Jewish Life

Week Three

☀ CELEBRATE YOUR GOOD ☀

IN WHICH YOU WILL GET CLEAR ABOUT WHO YOU ARE

❊ SING YOUR GOOD POINTS! ❊

"Collect your good points and make out of them a beautiful song."
❧ Rebbe Nachman of Breslov ❧

Acknowledging Your Special Talents & Strengths

This week, we will focus on identifying our talents, strengths and desires, and use them to elevate our service to G-d.

What makes you special? Each one of us has talents and strengths of our own. They are the special tools G-d has given us to accomplish our specific holy mission. This week, we'll focus on discovering and then harnessing our talents to serve G-d.

Sometimes we use them to serve one person; other times we use them to help many people, or to help ourselves. It's important to overcome our natural humility to assess what are the special qualities we were given to accomplish our unique mission in life. If you are ever depressed or feel like a failure, review this page to encourage yourself to keep going.

1. What are your special strengths, skills, and talents?
Put a star next to the ones you enjoy using, the ones that you use or learned because you really wanted to — not because someone else thought you should or because you needed them to survive:

*G-d gives us a talent to enjoy
so that we will enjoy helping others with it.*

2. What is unique about you, unlike anyone you know (or even slightly different)?

3. List at least five things that you enjoy doing:

    1.

    2.

    3.

    4.

    5.

4. What are the things you do best?

You are honorable.
You are special.

Be proud that YOU have the precious opportunity to Fulfill the Divine Will with your Talents.

בס"ד

Holy Sparks
www.HOLYSPARKS.COM
© 2017 Rae Shagalov

GET A NEW PERSPECTIVE ON YOURSELF

Interview Your Family And Friends

Sometimes our talents are so natural we don't even realize that others don't find them so easy. Often, those closest to us can see many of our good qualities that we are too modest to admit to ourselves. Ask those who have known you the best and the longest the questions below. Even if you think you know yourself pretty well, you might be surprised at how others perceive you.

1. What do you think is unique about me?

2.. What do you think are my talents, strengths, and skills?

3. What do you think I do especially well?

3. What do you like best about me?

4. If you could do something special with me, what would it be?

5. If you had the power to make me successful in one area, what area would you choose?

6. What do you think is my single greatest talent?

Explore Your Deepest Desires

"What is free will?
If you want, you do it, if you don't want, you don't do it."

Rebbe Nachman of Breslov – Likutey Moharan II, 110

Do you want to know who you are? Examine your deepest desires, the motivation to bring something into being from nothing. Ultimately, we do everything because we want to.

The first spark of thought is desire, the motivation to bring something into being from nothing. Ultimately, we do everything because we desire it. Desire is the clue G-d has implanted within us to guide us to our individual holy purpose. Desire provides the energy and motivation to continue achieving our purpose, despite all obstacles.

1. Things I really enjoy or things I really enjoy doing:

2. Things I would love to do, but haven't done yet (If only I could...)

3. Things I wish I could do well.

⟞⟝ STEP INTO YOUR DESIRE ⟞⟝

List below each of the things you identified that you wish were part of your life.
Think of one small step you could take toward satisfying your desire for it:

What you desire:

Example:
I wish I had more time to learn.

A small step you could take toward expressing your desire:

Example:
Learn five minutes on my lunch break.

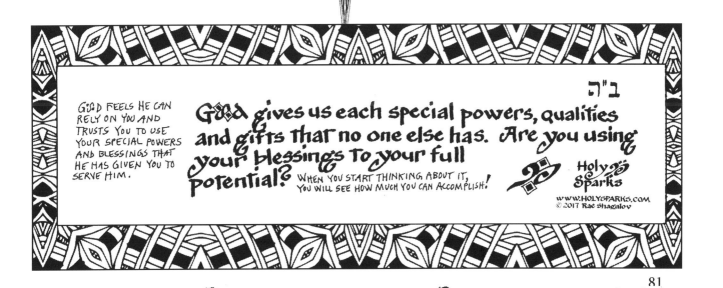

GOD FEELS HE CAN RELY ON YOU AND TRUSTS YOU TO USE YOUR SPECIAL POWERS AND BLESSINGS THAT HE HAS GIVEN YOU TO SERVE HIM.

ב"ה

G‑d gives us each special powers, qualities and gifts that no one else has. Are you using your blessings to your full potential? WHEN YOU START THINKING ABOUT IT, YOU WILL SEE HOW MUCH YOU CAN ACCOMPLISH!

Holy Sparks
WWW.HOLYSPARKS.COM
© 2017 Rae Shagalov

Test Your Desire

How do you know if your desire is coming from the side of holiness or the other side? Here's a simple test. For each desire, ask yourself:

1. Is this what G-d wants from me?

2. Will this bring me closer or farther away from G-d? How?

3. Is this going to bring out my potential? How?

4. Will it bring out the best in me? How?

5. How will it help others?

6. THE BIGGER TEST

How can you tell if you are fooling yourself by making up G-dly purposes for something that is not really so holy? It is always wise to ask someone whom you respect to help you decide if your desire is leading you closer or farther away from G-dliness. Think of someone whose judgment you trust. Ask that person's opinion about what you want. If you are still in doubt, ask the opinion of a second person whom you respect.

Are you an instrument of the Divine?

YOU WERE CREATED TO SERVE YOUR CREATOR!

Which is greater? Becoming good or doing good?

ב"ה

DESCENT FOR THE SAKE OF ASCENT

WE COME TO THIS WORLD TO PERFECT OURSELVES, SO THAT WHEN WE RETURN OUR SOULS, THEY ARE EVEN HIGHER THAN WHEN THEY CAME TO THIS WORLD. HOW DO WE PERFECT OURSELVES?

Ask yourself: What's in it for G-d?

G-d desires a dwelling place in this world... in you

IN THE WORLD OF MOSHIACH, THE FUTURE WORLD, THE TEMPLE WILL BE BUILT OF STONE. @ HUMILITY, SURRENDER TO G-DLINESS. EVERYTHING WE DO TO IMPROVE OURSELVES, IS FOR THE PURPOSE OF SERVING G-D.

Become good in order to do good.

NOT FOR YOURSELF, FOR G-D.

WHY DO YOU WANT TO FULFILL YOUR POTENTIAL? WHAT'S THE POINT? TO SERVE G-D!

G-d put the world inside of our heart

WITH WHAT DO WE SERVE G-D?

Wood @ OUR TALENTS, OUR POTENTIAL. WE HAVE THE ABILITY TO BE A DELICIOUS HUMAN BEING @ SEEDS • FRUITS

Stone @ SUBMISSION, DEVOTION, RESPONSIBILITY, COMMITMENT. LIFE IS NOT JUST ABOUT OURSELVES. ENDURING, CONSISTENT, STABLE, LOYAL.

Torah Mitzvahs REMODELS AND REFINES US. ACTION THAT TAKES US OUT OF OURSELVES. WE DO MITZVAHS PURELY TO SERVE OUR CREATOR BECAUSE WE ARE COMMANDED TO DO THEM.

BEING A STONE IS THE ART OF SILENCING ONESELF. SERVING, YES, SOMETIMES EVEN BEING TRAMPLED UPON. CREATING THE FOUNDATION OF HUMILITY UPON WHICH THE GREATEST OF DEEDS CAN BE BUILT.

Holy Sparks

PARSHAS VAYIGASH "PEACE AT LAST: IS MY LIFE ABOUT BEING ALL I CAN BE, OR TO BE SILENT AND SERVE MY CREATOR?"

Rabbi Reuven Wolf
5769

WWW.HOLYSPARKS.COM
© 2017 Rae Shagalov 22.1
UNEDITED NOTES

בס"ד

Serving G‑d means going beyond yourself.

The purpose of spirituality is to change your natural traits, and to change the nature of your traits. We are animalistic by nature. Our work is to refine our traits to become a mensch. But, even when we have refined our animal natures and become good human beings, we are still required to become even better people.

UNEDITED NOTES
TEACHER UNKNOWN
Holy Sparks
WWW.HOLYSPARKS.COM
© 2017 Rae Shagalov

⟩⟩ Become G-d's Partner in This World ⟨⟨

If you have received a talent from G-d, don't squander it! Use it for a G-dly purpose. How? By doing mitzvahs and serving others with our talents and strengths, we become G-d's partners in this world. G-d accomplishes everyday miracles through our efforts.

**Now that you have a better idea of your own special qualities....
How can you use your talents and strengths to improve:**

1. Yourself:

2. Your family life:

3. The community in which you live:

4. The community with which you worship:

5. Your workplace, school, or your child's or grandchild's school:

6. Your country:

7. Your World:

**What would you do
if you were chosen
to make a difference?**

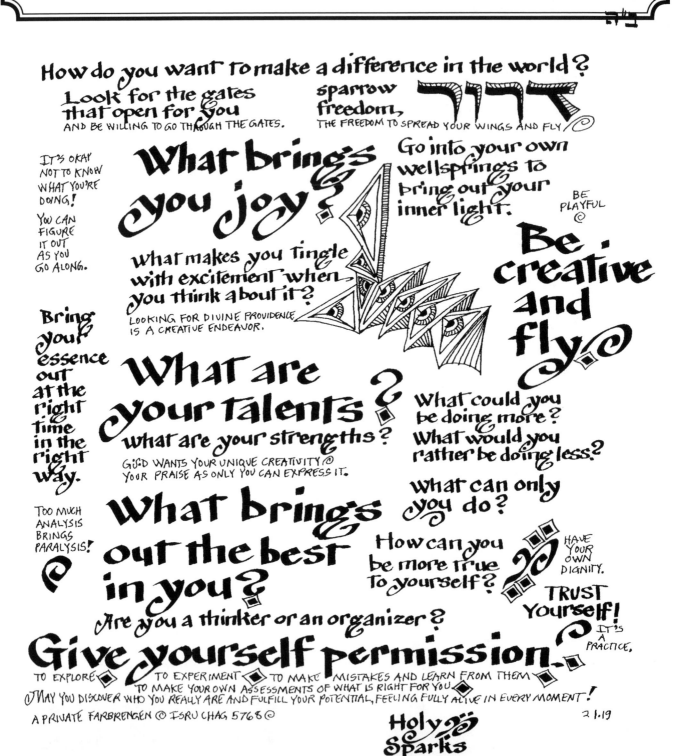

How do you want to make a difference in the world?

Look for the gates that open for you AND BE WILLING TO GO THROUGH THE GATES.

sparrow freedom, דרור THE FREEDOM TO SPREAD YOUR WINGS AND FLY

IT'S OKAY NOT TO KNOW WHAT YOU'RE DOING!

YOU CAN FIGURE IT OUT AS YOU GO ALONG.

What brings you joy?

Go into your own wellsprings to bring out your inner light.

BE PLAYFUL

What makes you tingle with excitement when you think about it?

LOOKING FOR DIVINE PROVIDENCE IS A CREATIVE ENDEAVOR.

Be creative and fly.

Bring your essence out at the right time in the right way.

What are your talents? what are your strengths?

G‑D WANTS YOUR UNIQUE CREATIVITY & YOUR PRAISE AS ONLY YOU CAN EXPRESS IT.

What could you be doing more? What would you rather be doing less?

what can only you do?

TOO MUCH ANALYSIS BRINGS PARALYSIS!

What brings out the best in you?

How can you be more true to yourself?

HAVE YOUR OWN DIGNITY.

TRUST Yourself! IT'S A PRACTICE.

Are you a thinker or an organizer?

Give yourself permission

TO EXPLORE ◆ TO EXPERIMENT ◆ TO MAKE MISTAKES AND LEARN FROM THEM ◆ TO MAKE YOUR OWN ASSESSMENTS OF WHAT IS RIGHT FOR YOU ◆

MAY YOU DISCOVER WHO YOU REALLY ARE AND FULFILL YOUR POTENTIAL, FEELING FULLY ALIVE IN EVERY MOMENT!

A PRIVATE FARBRENGEN @ ISRU CHAG 5768 @

2 1.19

Holy Sparks

Make a map to Geulah

Moshiach Action Plan

1. What talent or skill do you enjoy using?

2. What do you LOVE to do?

3. What kind of people do you enjoy being around? [family, older folks, children, special needs, etc.]

4. What are the problems, needs & wants of the kinds of people you enjoy?

5. What product or service could you happily create or offer with your talents, interests, strengths, or skills to help that person or group of people solve their problems or fill their lack?

6. What is one small action step you could take to get this started?

7. What is the soonest you could do this & who could help you?

www.HOLYSPARKS.com
© 2017 Rae Shagalov

Bring Moshiach with your Talents Today!

⚡ WRITE YOUR ETHICAL WILL ⚡

Today, you are going to create one of the most cherished gifts you can give to your family. You will clarify the values that are most important to you by writing an Ethical Will.

An Ethical will (Hebrew: "Tzava'ah") is a document designed to pass ethical values from one generation to the next. Ethical Wills can include personal, cultural, and spiritual values, hopes, experiences, advice, and your personal wisdom.

Think of all of the people connected to you who came before you. Think of all of those who will come after you. Put yourself in between. You are the active link in that chain. Write an Ethical Will bequeathing all of the values, qualities, personality traits, and goals you hold dear, to your loved ones and to all who will come after you in future generations.

1. What are the five most important values handed down to you by your ancestors, through your family, that you think that those who come after you should also treasure?

2. What Jewish values do you hold dear?

2. What other values from your life experience would you hand down to those who come after you?

ב"ה

Plant a value, and years later, harvest a grove of goodness.

Wherever you are, whatever you do, you are influencing those around you.

Take your next new step with JOY!

We are here to do!

Are you unified with your values? Have you integrated your values? Are you living your values?

What are my strengths?
How can I influence others?
How can I transform myself and those around me?
What values are you demonstrating every day of your life?
What is your vision?
What is your purpose?

Holy Sparks
WWW.HOLYSPARKS.COM
© 2017 Rae Shagalov

DR. BASYA PINSON "THE LEADER WITHIN" N'SHEI CHABAD SHEVAT
Rabbi Lawrence Keleman UNEDITED NOTES
V. 22.24

On the following page, or on a piece of stationery of your choice, write a letter addressed to your family, telling them about the values that you hold dear. The following sentence starters may help you structure the letter:

My hope/prayer for you is that you will always experience...

Treasure each day you have because...

Always remember...

Don't be afraid to...

Take good care of...

You may have tough times along the way, but I want to encourage you to...

I hope that you will find what makes you special and use it to...

I hope you will remember your heritage and pass on a legacy of...

Remember people in our family think it is important to always...

This is what I stand for...

Never take for granted...

Most importantly, my advice to you is...

Keep these beliefs at the center of your life...

Finally, I hope your life will be full of...

My Ethical Will

בס״ד

SOUL ADVENTURE ✦ DAY 21 ✦ (10 MINUTES)
✦ CREATE YOUR PERSONAL MISSION STATEMENT ✦

A mission statement is a concise statement of who you are and what you want to achieve every day, in every interaction. A mission statement includes your values, your talents, the people you serve, and your main goals that are consistent from day to day.

Your personal mission statement will clarify your purpose and give you a tool for defining all of your actions. It will remind you each day to focus your goals and activities on what is most important to you.

Creating a personal mission statement can take a while to develop because you are defining the essence of your actions every day and your goals for your whole life.

Today, you will create a first draft of your mission statement, but it may take you several weeks or even months before you feel that it is a complete and concise expression of your innermost values and directions. Even then, you will want to review it regularly and make minor changes as the years and changing circumstances bring additional insights.

Describe your personal mission statement in the present tense as if you were reporting what you actually see, hear, think and feel after your ideal outcome has been realized.

A mission statement should answer the following two questions:

1. What do I want to contribute to this world every day through all of my actions?

2. What do I stand for?

Review your Ethical Will for ideas.

ב"ה

You matter to the One who matters most.

Birth is G‑d's statement that you matter!

YOU ARE IMPORTANT, IRREPLACABLE, INVALUABLE. HOW DO YOU KNOW? BECAUSE YOU EXIST. WHAT YOU ARE HERE TO DO, NO ONE ELSE WHO HAS EVER LIVED OR WHO WILL EVER LIVED CAN REPLACE YOU OR DO WHAT YOU AND ONLY YOU WERE CREATED TO DO.

MAY WE MERIT THAT WE NO LONGER HAVE TO STRUGGLE. MAY WE HAVE THE STRENGTH TO MAINTAIN OUR VISION.

RABBI SIMON JACOBSON

Holy Sparks

Now, create an action statement from your answers to the first two questions. Include your main talent as the vehicle through which you accomplish your mission and identify whom you serve.

Keep it brief, simple to understand, and easy to memorize.

Here's a Formula for Your Mission Statement

Your core value statement PLUS

What you want to contribute PLUS

Your special talents = Your Mission Statement

Here are some sample personal mission statements:

"Growing from strength to strength, I inspire my family to achieve their full potential in Torah and mitzvahs, through my acts of lovingkindness every day."

"My mission is to help children grow intellectually, emotionally, and spiritually by showing them G-d's loving involvement in the details of their lives through my love of science."

"Learning from everything that happens, every day, I inspire everyone I meet with my trust in G-d, and with my talent for healing, by revealing the goodness that is concealed in every situation."

"I elevate the divine sparks in everything I do by looking for G-d's presence in everything I experience and everyone I meet."

Memorize your mission statement, and review it every morning so that you can infuse it in all of the decisions and actions of your day. Feel free to expand and refine your mission statement as you grow and refine yourself.

My Mission Statement

בס״ד

⊙ ⸎ On Shabbos After Candle Lighting.. ⸎ ⊙

On Friday night, after candlelighting, sit by the flames for a few minutes and re-experience your Joy Meditation. Shabbos is a joyful vacation with G-d.

Imagine again that the time of Redemption has arrived and the whole world is filled with joy. Moshiach, the Redeemer for whom we have all been waiting, is here at last. There is no more pain or suffering. This is the first moment of Geulah, the era when all G-dliness is revealed, when the whole world is surrounded by goodness and filled with kindness.

The joyful purpose that was hidden in every hurtful thing in the world since the beginning of time is now revealed. The world is fully at peace. Imagine vividly what this joyful world is like. Over Shabbos, ask your family and friends to share their wishes, hopes and dreams. Ask them what values are important to them and share your insights with them.

Melavah Malkah

⊙ ⸎ After You See Three Stars in Three Different Parts of the Sky ⸎ ⊙

Melavah Malka means "Escorting the Queen." The evening after the Sabbath (Saturday night) is a special spiritual time for the soul to enjoy the lingering holiness of Shabbos and bring it into the week with encouraging words, stories of righteous people (especially the Baal Shem Tov), Torah thoughts and holy songs. It's also customary to have hot drinks (made with fresh water from the faucet) and delicious bread.

After Havdalah, the ritual for separating the Holy Sabbath from the rest of the week, record any insights you might have had over Shabbos.

Gather your family or friends together for a Melavah Malka Farbrengen (Gathering) with a focus of sharing your dreams, talents and stories.

As you share with each other encouraging words, Torah thoughts and stories, each person can also mention what he or she hopes and dreams for in the coming week or year. Then you and everyone present can make a blessing to help each person connect their hopes and dreams to G-d's will and answer with a heartfelt "Amen."

On Shabbos we experience the kiss of G‑d.

Teshuva
Return
Returning to your essence, connecting to your soul

בס"ד

Rebbetzin Esther Jungreis

Holy Sparks www.HOLYSPARKS.COM
©1990-2016 Rae Shagalov

Create Your Joyfully Jewish Life

Week Four

☀ TESHUVA ☀

IN WHICH YOU WILL TRANSFORM FAILURE INTO SUCCESS

RETURNING TO G-D

If you want a spiritual experience, you have to do the work.

The 4 "R's" of Teshuva

1. Recognize that what you did was wrong.

2. Regret what you did wholeheartedly.

3. Resolve not to do it again.

4. Refrain from making the same mistake when faced with the same situation.

"Teshuva" means "Return" – returning to the path of G-dliness. Our Sages teach us that when we do Teshuva, we rectify our mistakes. We actually fix and uplift all previous mistakes of the same nature and restore the holiness of our being. In this way, bit by bit, we restore the entire world to holiness.

At the heart of Teshuva is the faith that no human action is irreversible. It's a renewal of the creation of our life-force, bringing more G-dliness down from the source.

Teshuva is how we cleanse our soul if, G-d forbid, we have dragged her into unclean thoughts or deeds. We all have a certain standard for how clean our homes have to be. We also have to determine our spiritual standards – How pure can we make our soul? What needs to be discarded? What needs to be scrubbed? What polished?

בס"ד

Teshuva

The 4 Steps of Teshuva

- **Recognize** that what you did was wrong.

- **Regret** what you did wholeheartedly.

- **Resolve** not to do it ever again.

- **Refrain** from doing that thing the next time you are faced with the same situation!

THE LONGER YOU REFRAIN, THE LESS THAT TEMPTATION WILL BOTHER YOU, UNTIL EVENTUALLY IT CEASES TO BE A DIFFICULT ISSUE.

Holy Sparks
WWW.HOLYSPARKS.COM
© 2017 Rae Shagalov

☉⤙ Teshuva is a search for truth. ⤚☉

Real Teshuva is finding one thing that is not right in yourself, one thing you can really, truly change. Every person has the strength to change.

Don't become discouraged. The Harsh Inner Critic sometimes says, "Who are you fooling? You'll never change! Don't even bother to try — you've failed a million times before!"

Tell your Inner Voice: "Thank you for your opinion, but I can change, and with G-d's help, I WILL change." Every single little bit of Teshuva counts. Never underestimate what you can accomplish with your effort!

Over the next few days, you'll have some fun tools to use to help you choose something small — one thing you would like to change in yourself. You can use these tools and strategies to work on that one thing, a little bit every day, for just a few minutes - for a whole year. I promise, if you do this, you will see progress in your spiritual and personal growth!

☉⤙ What You'll Do ⤚☉

⟡ Time for a Powerful Pause ⟡

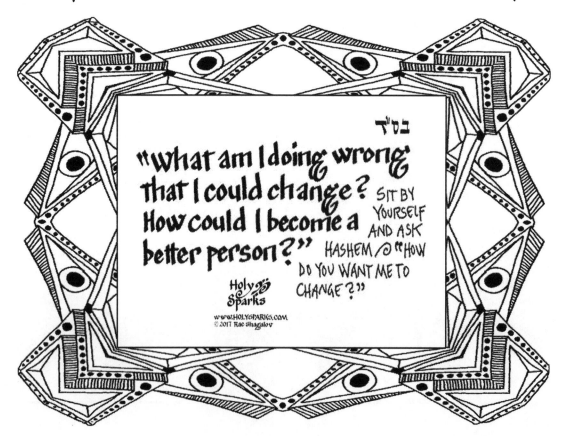

ב"ה

Every person, no matter what they've done, can do teshuva.

How to do Teshuva:

Say to G‑d:

"I'm sorry for what I did. I wish that I had never done it."

then don't do it anymore!

DON'T BE AFRAID TO DO TESHUVA! DON'T BE AFRAID TO CHANGE! DON'T BE AFRAID TO TAKE THE NEXT STEP!

Holy Sparks

☀ ALIGN YOUR ACTIONS WITH YOUR PURPOSE ☀

❧ Don't Shoot the Bears! ❧

This is a true story.

There is a small town in a rural area that has a beautiful zoo, but it wasn't always as nice as it is now. Years ago it was just a bunch of concrete and chain link fenced-in pens holding wild animals.

Gradually the zoo began to upgrade the enclosures to make them look like more natural environments. When it came time to remodel the largest exhibit, the zoo planned a beautiful bear grotto with a running stream, trees, and a cave.

But they had a problem. What would they do with the bears while they were remodeling their home?

The Director of the zoo came up with a very simple solution. He shot the bears. Although this was a very efficient solution, it was rather short-sighted. Very soon after, the zoo not only had new bears but also a new director.

Once we have a clear vision and an action plan for creating our ideal world, it is very important that we make sure that every action is infused and aligned with the essence of our purpose. This is called integrity.

Every time you make a choice, ask yourself:

Will this choice reflect my values and mission?

Is this in alignment with what G-d wants for me?"

⊙⤙ What You'll Do ⤚⊙

⤜ Review Your Ethical Will & Your Mission Statement ⤛

Are there any choices that you have made or are making that
conflict with your values or your mission in life? In the left column,
list your values conflicts. In the right column, decide what you can do
to realign your actions with your values.

What action or decision have you made that is in conflict with your mission or values?

What can you do to realign it?

בס"ד

"The Voice of My Beloved Calls Out to Me."

Sometimes we feel too damaged to return to G‑d.

THERE IS A CORE AND ESSENCE IN EACH OF US THAT IS COMPLETELY HOLY, PURE AND WHOLE. THIS HOLY SPARK IS PART OF G‑D AND ACCOMPANIES US EVERYWHERE, EVEN INTO THE DARKEST PLACES OF OUR SOUL.

The moment a person calls out to G‑d to ask to come closer to G‑d, G‑d gives us the strength to return, AND LOVES AND ACCEPTS US AS IF WE HAD NEVER CAUSED A BLEMISH ON OUR SOULS.

תשובה

WALK HUMBLY WITH YOUR G‑D.

YOU SHALL KNOW G‑D IN ALL YOUR WAYS.

LOVE YOUR FELLOW AS YOUR SELF.

I PLACE G‑D BEFORE ME CONSTANTLY.

YOU SHALL BE WHOLE WITH G‑D.

When we do something good, that good that we do is drawn up after a greater, more integrated good.

HOW CAN WE CREATE THE ENERGY WE WILL NEED TO DO TESHUVA?

Be G‑d Oriented.

Everything we do has the potential to be uplifted, to be Holy, to become part of the G‑dly tapestry of Creation.

There is a deep longing and yearning of G‑d to be re-united with His children.

Old schmutz is not the same as new schmutz. WHY WOULD PEOPLE WAIT IN LONG LINES OVER AND OVER AGAIN TO GET THEIR CARS WASHED WHEN THEY ARE JUST GOING TO DRIVE THEM INTO THE SCHMUTZ AND GET THEM DIRTY ALL OVER AGAIN? BECAUSE OLD SCHMUTZ WILL CORRODE AND DESTROY THE CAR IF IT'S LEFT THERE. SO IT IS WITH OUR SOULS. WHEN WE DO A SIN THAT STAINS OUR SOUL, WE HAVE TO CLEANSE IT IMMEDIATELY BEFORE IT CAUSES MORE DAMAGE, AND CLEANSE IT OFTEN TO PREVENT DAMAGE.

Holy Sparks
WWW.HOLYSPARKS.COM
© 2017 Rae Shagalov

Take a quiet moment and ask yourself:

"Is this what I want to be doing with my life?" CREATE A MOMENT OF CLARITY!

WALK IN THAT WHICH IS CONCEALED DEEPLY IN YOUR HEART AND LISTEN FOR THE ECHO OF G‑D.

RABBI MICHEL TWERSKI
RABBI LEIB KELEMAN

"Hashem Is Pleading; How Do We Respond?" Selichos 5762

• JEWISH AWARENESS AMERICA • JEWISH LEARNING EXCHANGE •

UNEDITED NOTES 16:76

⇥ PUT YOUR JEWISH GUILT TO WORK ⇤

⟿ Using Guilt & Regret to Grow ⟻

Jewish guilt - It's the punchline of so many Jewish jokes, usually involving Jewish mothers and always involving unmet expectations. But Jewish guilt is more than just a sterotype. It's a powerful tool for refining our souls and increasing our happiness and success in life.

Guilt is such a useful tool precisely because it makes us feel so uncomfortable. Rabbi Abraham Twerski, a chassidic psychiatrist, uses the following metaphor:

The lobster is a soft animal that lives in a rigid shell. As the lobster grows, that shell becomes very confining, and the lobster feels itself under pressure and uncomfortable. What does it do? It goes under a rock to protect itself, casts off the shell, and produces a new one. Well, eventually, that shell becomes very uncomfortable, too, as the lobster continues to grow. Back under the rocks it goes to shed the shell, again and again.

Guilty feelings are those uncomfortable feelings that tell us that the shell of our old selves is too confining. They are signals that something is wrong and some action needs to be taken so that we can continue to grow. If we feel guilty and don't act to change what is wrong, the guilt could turn into action-suppressing depression or avoidance.

When we examine the source of our feelings of guilt and identify where we've gone astray, this journey of the heart naturally leads to feelings of regret. If you truly feel there is nothing you can do about the situation, then you can ask G-d to forgive you and guide you in making up for your mistake. But first, let's see how we can transform guilt and regret into positive, corrective action.

WE ARE VESSELS OF HOLINESS

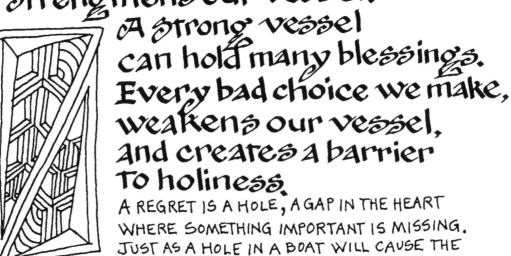

Every choice we make to do good, strengthens our vessel. A strong vessel can hold many blessings. Every bad choice we make, weakens our vessel, and creates a barrier to holiness.

A REGRET IS A HOLE, A GAP IN THE HEART WHERE SOMETHING IMPORTANT IS MISSING. JUST AS A HOLE IN A BOAT WILL CAUSE THE BOAT TO SINK, REGRETS EVOKE IN US A SINKING FEELING, A FEELING OF LOSS. IF WE DON'T TAKE ACTION TO CORRECT THE LACK THAT THE REGRET LEAVES BEHIND, THE VESSEL OF HOLINESS WE ARE BUILDING WITH OUR POSITIVE ACTIONS, BEGINS TO LEAK.

1. For the next five minutes, write down everything you regret doing or not doing in your life so far. If only I had/had not...

Holy Sparks
9.46
www.HOLYSPARKS.com
© 2017 Rae Shagalov

⊙ᴗ᷈ What You'll Do ᷈ᴗ⊙

Is there anything you feel guilty about? For every guilty feeling, write down something you could do tomorrow to correct what you've done wrong.

Then do it! Feel the new energy that this positive action restores to you.

1. I feel guilty that:

2. This is what I should have done:

3. This is what I could do tomorrow to correct it:

It's never too late to change.

We have a life that is meaningful. We have a purpose that is holy. We feel guilty when we do other things that lead us away from serving Hashem. THIS IS THE WAY THE JEW IS MADE.

Torah Umesorah
MIDWINTER PRINCIPALS CONFERENCE 18,72
LOS ANGELES

☀ CHOOSE ONE SMALL THING TO CHANGE ☀

OK. Now it's time to choose.

What is one small change you want to make in yourself for your personal and spiritual growth? Write it below. Color in the frame and visualize yourself being successful with this goal. Go back to Day 12 and use the Baby Step tool to break your goal down into smaller steps.

With G-d's help, I am going to change this one thing.

בס"ד

Holy Sparks
www.HOLYSPARKS.COM
© 2017 Rae Shagalov

When you are determined, you will win.

Awaken the desire in your heart. Ask the Master of the universe to help you. Choose one thing to change and focus on it every day.

When you fail or fall, just pick yourself up and begin again.

You have to really want it. You have to really want to change.

It is difficult to change, But you can do it!

"Master of the Universe! Help me to overcome this!"

Choose one small thing.

You CAN change! How? What you want you do. Say, "I want to _____." What you desire you will acquire.

Holy Sparks
www.HOLYSPARKS.COM
© 2017 Rae Shagalov

Teshuva IS THE RETURN TO THE ESSENTIAL SELF. IT DOESN'T JUST MEAN TAKING ON A NEW RESOLUTION. IT ALSO MEANS DOING SOMETHING THAT YOU ARE ALREADY DOING, AND DOING IT EVEN BETTER IN A SPECIAL WAY.

Pray and meditate every day, and ask G-d to help you change this one thing. If you wronged another person, take courage and ask the person you have hurt to forgive you. If that's not possible, ask G-d to forgive you with your whole heart.

Crying is an integral part of doing Teshuva. If you truly regret what you did wrong, you cannot help but cry. Your tears will cleanse your soul and are stored and treasured in Heaven.

On the 28th day, we'll further explore the mystical world of prayer. Tomorrow we'll open the channel of success with our Super Spiritual Power of Mitzvhahs.

111

TO CONCEIVE OF IDEAS: FAITH

The point

OUR VALUE SYSTEM

The Plan

OUR EMOTIONS HOW WE EXPERIENCE THE WORLD

THOUGHT, SPEECH AND ACTION

HOW WE INTERACT WITH THE WORLD.

We have one thing G‑d doesn't have / CONFUSION

Connect your gifts back to the Source.

In this world we see the creation, not the Creator. G‑D DOESN'T "EXIST," G‑D CREATES EXISTENCE. **G‑d creates us every single second.**

EVERY "I" IS DIFFERENT.

EACH PERSON HAS ONE SPECIAL QUALITY THAT NO ONE ELSE HAS. MOSES WAS THE MOST HUMBLE MAN WHO EVER LIVED. WHY? MOSES HAD THE SPECIAL QUALITY OF SEEING THE GOOD IN EVERYONE. HE SAW THE SPECIAL, UNIQUE QUALITY THAT EACH PERSON HAD. MOSES SAW 3,000,000 QUALITIES THAT OTHER PEOPLE HAD THAT HE DIDN'T HAVE, AND THAT MADE HIM HUMBLE.

The Jewish Feeling ~ the Pintele Yid

TESHUVA IS RETURNING THE LETTER HEY, RETURNING ALL OF OUR QUALITIES AND ALL OF OUR TALENTS TO G‑D.

THE ESSENCE OF THE JEW IS TO THANK G‑D FOR EVERYTHING.

EACH PERSON HAS CERTAIN TESTS AND IS GIVEN THE STRENGTH AND SPECIAL ABILITIES HE OR SHE WILL NEED TO MASTER THE TEST.

What are your special tests and abilities? How can you return them to G‑d?

TESHUVA FROM THE LOWER FEAR OF G‑D: "WHAT'S GOING TO HAPPEN TO ME?"

TESHUVA FROM THE LOWER LOVE OF G‑D: "I LOVE WHAT G‑D DOES FOR ME."

The way to help the whole world is to do Teshuva ~ Return to G‑d

WHO ARE YOU RIGHT NOW?

Make the world a better place, starting with yourself. How? Return your best qualities to G‑d.

DON'T UNDERESTIMATE THE TREMENDOUS POTENTIAL AND POWERFUL EFFECT THAT EACH THING THAT YOU DO HAS ON THE WORLD.

Be who you really are in a really happy way.
THIS IS THE BEST TESHUVA OF ALL!

TESHUVA FROM THE UPPER LOVE: "G‑D IS REALLY GOOD."

TESHUVA FROM THE UPPER FEAR: "I DON'T UNDERSTAND ANYTHING; I JUST WANT TO SERVE G‑D."

To be a Jew in this world is the greatest miracle of all.

Heard from: Rabbi Tuvia Bolton 1 Tishrei 5768

Holy Sparks
WWW.HOLYSPARKS.COM
© 2017 Rae Shagalov
BAIS CHANA OF CALIFORNIA
WOMEN'S YESHIVA 17TH ANNIVERSARY

21.15

UNEDITED NOTES

ב"ה

We laugh because we know, we see before our eyes that our prophecies are coming TRUE!

WE ARE WITNESSING THE FOOTSTEPS OF MOSHIACH!

How good it is to be a Jew!

When we live with faith and meaning in life, then we can be happy through the "oys" as well as the joys of life.

We may not know on which path G‑d is taking us, but we can be happy that G‑d loves us enough to lead us on the path.

WE DON'T GLORIFY PAIN AND SUFFERING. WE DON'T SEEK MARTYRDOM; WE HAVE NO DEATH WISHES.

We sanctify life!

In the midst of the tears, a ROARING Laugh

"The Joy and Oy of Being a Jew."

RABBI MOSHE BRYSKI
UNEDITED NOTES

Holy Sparks

JLI National Jewish Retreat 5776

THE MITZVAHS

ARE THE CORE & ESSENCE OF G-D.

WHEN WE DO THE MITZVAHS,

WE DRAW G-D INTO OURSELVES

AND INTO OUR WORLD.

Our 6th spiritual power tool is the Mitzvah. How can this, the lowest of all worlds, become the highest of all worlds? Through doing the mitzvahs, we use physical objects to perform G-d's will, thereby connecting us to G-d.

By donating a dollar, lighting Shabbos candles, eating Kosher food, refraining from doing evil, and by doing any of the 613 mitzvahs from the Torah, we bring G-d's essence to the world. In this way we strengthen and elevate the physical world so that it can fully receive the infinite revelation of G-d.

Maimonides writes that a person should always see himself and the entire world as equally balanced between good and evil. With just one positive deed, one can tip the balance and bring salvation to the entire world. The Lubavitcher Rebbe, Rabbi Menachem M. Schneerson, declared, " Moshiach is ready to come. All that we have to do, is add in acts of Goodness and Kindness." Maybe the final act of goodness that tips the scale to Redemption will be yours!

Mitzvah is a Hebrew word which means "commandment" and "connection." The Mitzvahs are G-d's commandments to the Jewish people in the Torah. There are 613 mitzvahs - 613 holy sparks or strands of divine light through which Jews can connect to G-d, and seven mitzvahs for non-Jews*. One of the constant mitzvahs is to "love G-d." One of the ways we do this is by using all of our energy and talents to serve G-d. Today, we're going to focus on one mitzvah and make it shine.

THE SOUL IS SO EXCITED TO COME TO THIS WORLD TO DO MITZVAHS!

*See page 146 for the 7 mitzvahs for righteous gentiles

HASHEM, TODAY I BEGIN CLINGING TO YOU.

BEGIN YOUR MEDITATION WITH THESE WORDS EVERY DAY.

G‑D WANTS YOU TO HAVE EVERYTHING GOOD SPIRITUALLY & MATERIALLY.

G‑D IS IN THE DETAILS.

EVERYTHING IN PRAYER HAS A PRICE & DON'T STOP PRAYING! YOUR NEXT PRAYER MIGHT BE THE LAST PAYMENT.

R. VELVEL HESHIN

WHAT IS A MITZVAH?

G‑D's WISDOM CONTRACTED INTO HUMAN ACTION.

HOW DO WE APPROACH G‑D?

EVERYTHING COMES FROM G‑D. WE CAN'T EVEN CLAIM OUR NEXT BREATH AS OUR OWN! SO ASK HASHEM FOR EVERYTHING.

Through the mitzvot.

Don't hold back ASK FOR EVERYTHING! BUT FIRST, THANK G‑D FOR EVERYTHING. THE KINDNESS OF HASHEM IS INFINITE.

Before there can be peace on the outside There has to be peace on the inside. REB NACHMAN

EVERYTHING IS LITTLE BY LITTLE.

WHERE IS THE KINGDOM OF G‑D? In the keeping of the law. WHERE IS THE LIGHT OF MOSHIACH? In the Halacha.

YOU CAN'T HAVE A RELATIONSHIP WITH G‑D IF YOU DON'T COMMUNICATE WITH HIM. TALK TO HASHEM TODAY!

Holy Sparks

www.HOLYSPARKS.COM © 2017 Rae Shagalov

R. Ozer Bergman of Breslov Research Institute

at Happy Minyan

JERUSALEM UNEDITED NOTES

✳ DO A NEW MITZVAH ✳

"You shall love the Lord your God with all your heart, with all your soul, and with all your might."

· Deut. 6:5 ·

We hug G-d through our mitzvahs

Mitzvahs are food for the soul. The Mitzvahs are a medium through which we can become aware of our own soul. 613 Mitzvahs are 613 ways to perfect your soul!

G-d loves us with an infinite love. But how can that infinite love fit into little, tiny, finite us? G-d constricted His endless love without end for us and His infinite wisdom into the mitzvahs. When we do a mitzvah, we cause G-d's hidden love to descend and become revealed in this world.

Every time we do a Mitzvah, we create an angel, a positive force in ourselves and in the world. We draw down G-d's infinite light into this world and refine the world so that G-d can dwell here in the revealed G-dly light right in the midst of our lives!

So, today, we're going to do a new mitzvah, one we don't usually do or a mitzvah that we do but want to reinvigorate with new light and energy by doing it in a new way.

In order to be successful, take small steps. Start with a mitzvah that is easy for you. Break down the harder things into small do-able parts with the Baby Steps Tool (Day 12).

You want to stop speaking Lashon Hara (gossip)? Start with 10 minutes a day. You want to give Tzedakah? Start by putting a penny in the Pushke (charity box) every day. Little by little, we fill our world with G-dliness.

בס"ד

Every mitzvah that we do is like giving a gift to the Ribono Shel Olam.* If you were giving a gift to someone you especially honored, you would choose it carefully, wrap it beautifully, send it special delivery.

ENJOY THE MITZVAHS.

HANDLE THE MITZVAHS WITH CARE!

IN THE GIFT BOX, WRITE THE NEW MITZVAH YOU WILL DO OR THE MITZVAH YOU'RE ALREADY DOING THAT YOU WANT TO DO IN A NEW WAY.

*MASTER OF THE UNIVERSE

Holy Sparks
WWW.HOLYSPARKS.COM
© 2017 Rae Shagalov

בס"ד

The mitzvahs were given in order to refine humanity

Through the mitzvahs, we create a relationship with G○d by becoming G○dlike◆

The mitzvahs reveal G○dliness in every aspect of the world, every moment of time, and in the character of the people who do the mitzvahs◆

When you give, you become a giver◆

The mitzvahs tell us: "Ask not what others can do for you; ask what you can do for others◆"

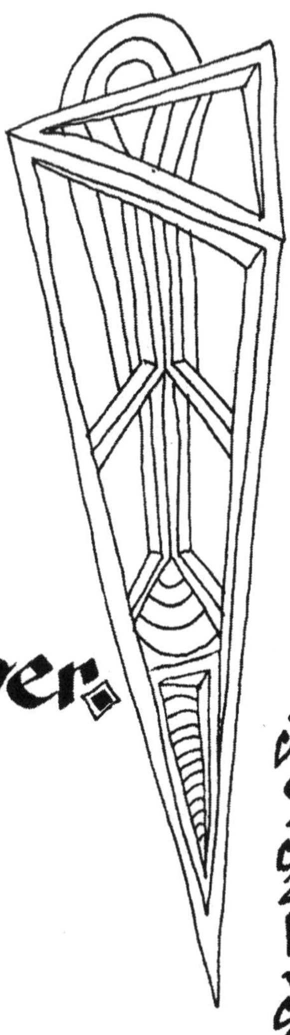

THE MITZVAHS JOIN US TO A HIGHER LEVEL OF MEANING AND TO A HIGHER LEVEL OF REALITY◆

The mitzvahs reveal the name of G○d in the world◆

How do we make mitzvah more meaningful? Make them central to your life and the lives of your children◆

Rabbi Mordechai Becher Ohr Somayach

Holy Sparks

From the farthest point to the ultimate closeness...

Moshiach is a revelation, not a revolution.

IN THE DAYS OF MOSHIACH, WE WILL NOT BE ABLE TO DO THE MITZVAHS ANY MORE, BUT WE WILL EXPERIENCE ALL OF THE G‑DLINESS THAT WAS BROUGHT DOWN THROUGH THE MILLIONS OF MITZVAHS WE PERFORMED THROUGHOUT THE ENTIRE GOLUS:

IN THESE DAYS WE PERFORM THE MITZVAHS, AND THROUGH THE MITZVAHS, WE BRING DOWN G‑DLINESS. WE CAN DO THIS, BUT WE CANNOT EXPERIENCE IT.

The mitzvahs accumulate into Infinity

WHAT IS A MITZVAH? THE DEEPEST, INNER-MOST INTIMATE DESIRE OF G‑D.

Through the doing of the mitzvahs, we draw down the Infinite Light of G‑dliness and connect this Infinite Light to every aspect of creation.

This is a designer world.

THROUGH THE OBJECTS OF THIS WORLD, WHICH WERE CREATED SOLELY FOR THE SAKE OF THE MITZVAHS, WE DRAW THE INFINITE LIGHT FROM ABOVE, DOWN INTO OUR WORLD. THE OBJECT WAS TRAPPED IN A KLIPPAH, A SHELL OF UNHOLINESS, AND THROUGH THE MITZVAH, IS CONNECTED TO HOLINESS, ELEVATED FROM THE LOWEST, FARTHEST POINT TO THE ULTIMATE CLOSENESS.

G‑d created a space in which He is completely concealed.

AND IN THIS SPACE, HE CREATED MANY WORLDS. IN THIS SPACE G‑D INJECTED, SO TO SAY, A SMALL RAY OF HIS INFINITE LIGHT TO CREATE THESE WORLDS, EACH WORLD RECEIVING LESS AND LESS LIGHT, LESS AND LESS G‑DLY ENERGY, UNTIL, AT LAST, HE CREATED OUR WORLD. THEN, IN THIS DARKEST CORNER OF ALL THE WORLDS, WE REACH OUT TO THE INFINITE LIGHT FROM OUR LEAST OF ALL REALITIES, AND DO A MITZVAH, AND RELEASE THE ULTIMATE ESSENCE OF G‑D INTO ALL OF THE WORLDS & REALITIES.

Some things were created for us to deny.

UNKOSHER THINGS HAVE A KLIPPAH, A SHELL SO THICK, WE CANNOT ELEVATE THEM. THEY WERE CREATED FOR US TO BUILD WITHIN OURSELVES THE STRENGTH TO SAY NO TO THEM.

A penny in the Tzedakah box contains more G‑dly energy than all of the angels in the cosmos.

Rabbi R. Wolf
UNEDITED NOTES

CHAPTER 37
Tanya   Jan. 3, 5760

Holy Sparks

WWW.HOLYSPARKS.COM
© 2017 Rae Shagalov

✦ THE HEALING POWER OF FORGIVENESS ✦

Difficult people are sent to your life to help you develop your inner strength of giving and understanding. You cannot change other people, but when you change yourself, others change in response to you.

So, how do you change yourself when you're feeling resentful or hurt? Connect to the little point of G-d in yourself, and connect that little point of G-d to the little point of G-d in others.

Do you forgive easily? Do you give everyone the benefit of the doubt? Do you forgive yourself? What was, was! It's done, finished, over. Let it go! Forgive and start all over again. If this is hard, the One Minute Miracle Meditation can help. When you breathe out, release the resentment and hurt.

But what about when we hurt others? The more you hurt a person, the harder it is to ask someone for forgiveness

If we hurt someone in any way, we are obligated to ask for forgiveness, and we are also obligated to forgive when asked. One has to ask for forgiveness up to three times. We can forgive because we like to be good. An even higher level is to forgive because we care for the other person who needs our forgiveness.[1]

Just say, "I'm so sorry. I made a mistake. Please forgive me for what I did."

⊙ ᴠ WHAT YOU'LL DO ᴠ ⊙

Take courage. Ask the people you have hurt to forgive you. On the next page is a coloring page you can use to write a Forgiveness Note. Choose someone whom you might have hurt. While you color in the page, think of the person in a loving way and write a personal message from your heart in the empty spaces or on the back. Then, give or mail it to the person.

[1]Heard from Rabbi Reuven Wolf

ב"ה

Remember all of the good.
Say:

To your mother
To your father
To your brother
To your sister
To your uncle
To your aunt
To your child

To your husband
To your ex-husband
To your wife
To your ex-wife

I FORGIVE YOU

THESE ARE THE WORDS THAT WILL BRING MOSHIACH!

TO YOUR NEPHEW
TO YOUR NIECE
TO YOUR NEIGHBOR
YOUR LAWYER
YOUR STOCKBROKER
YOUR DOCTOR
YOUR ROOMMATE
YOUR COUSIN

To your friend
To your enemy
To your business partner

TO YOUR TEACHER
YOUR STUDENT
TO YOUR BOSS

TO YOUR GRANDMOTHER
TO YOUR GRANDFATHER
TO YOUR GRANDCHILD

Say the words: "I forgive you," And be free!

TO YOUR FIANCE'
TO YOUR EX-FIANCE'
TO YOUR RABBI
TO YOUR MOTHER-IN-LAW
YOUR FATHER-IN-LAW
YOUR DAUGHTER-IN-LAW
YOUR SON-IN-LAW

Expand your generosity of spirit.

Tisha B'Av 5759   Rabbi Frand   CHOFETZ CHAIM FOUNDATION VIDEO '97

UNEDITED NOTES

Holy Sparks

בס"ד

סליחה
Forgive

◆ Reflect
HOW ARE YOUR REACTIONS
AFFECTING YOUR WELL-BEING?

◆ Release
THE ARAMAIC WORD FOR "FORGIVE"
LITERALLY MEANS TO "UNTIE."
UNTIE THE BINDINGS AND LOOSEN
YOURSELF FROM THAT PERSON'S MISDEED.

Forgiving is freeing yourself
from the chain of pain that
connects you to that person.

◆ Recharge your faith
REMEMBER
THAT G‑D IS
IN CHARGE OF
THE WORLD, AND
HAS CREATED THIS SITUATION SO THAT
YOU CAN SERVE AT YOUR HIGHEST
LEVEL. BY BRINGING OUT YOUR INNERMOST
STRENGTH, YOU CAN FIX AND REFINE THIS
PARTICULAR DARKNESS IN THE WORLD,
WITH YOUR INNER LIGHT.

◆ Realize
THE ANGER YOU FEEL TOWARD
THE PERSON WHO HURT YOU
HARMS YOU, NOT THE OTHER.
IT TAKES UP VALUABLE SPACE
IN YOUR EMOTIONS THAT COULD
BE USED TO HELP AND HEAL.

◆ Revenge
The best revenge
is living, well!
Turn the
darkness
into tremendous
light in your life.

IDENTIFY 10 POSITIVE OUTCOMES
OF THIS EXPERIENCE.

Holy Sparks

WWW.HOLYSPARKS.COM
© 2017 Rae Shagalov

The 5 R's of Forgiveness

YOUR 7TH SPIRITUAL POWER TOOL
⚡ PRAYER ⚡

"In prayer we stand on our tiptoes and give G-d a kiss."

❦ Rabbi Reuven Wolf ❦

Tefilah is the process by which we begin looking inward at ourselves. We proceed to focus on G-d and bring ourselves close to Him by raising ourselves above the mundane life that prevails during the rest of the day.

In Hebrew, the word for prayer is tefilah. What does the word tefilah mean? The word tefilah comes from the word pallel which means "to judge."

Tefilah is a time of self-evaluation, self-judgment, and introspection. It's a time to focus within. What do I need? What am I all about? What are my faults? What are my good qualities? What do I need from G-d, and why G-d should give it to me?

On another level, in another translation, tefilah means "attachment." When we pray, we create a bond between ourselves and our Creator. Prayer is a process of putting things together. When we pray, there are only two things in the universe, G-d and ourselves.

בס"ד

WHEN WE PRAY TO HAKADOSH BARUCH HU START OFF WITH PRAISES AND END OFF WITH THANKFULNESS, AND IN BETWEEN, WE ASK FOR WHAT WE NEED.

Before you pray, always praise G-d. Afterwards thank G-d.

Holy Sparks
WWW.HOLYSPARKS.ORG
©2001-2014 Rae Shagalov

Drawing G‑d down into your life

G‑D MEETS US DOWN HERE.

A DIVINE LIGHT SHOWERS DOWN ON YOUR SOUL. WE ASSIMILATE THIS DIVINE LIGHT INTO OUR SOULS WHEN WE LEARN TORAH.

620 PILLARS OF LIGHT! CONNECTING HEAVEN TO EARTH.

into your world.

G‑d descends to envelop you. In Torah & mitzvahs, G‑d hugs and kisses us.

A MITZVAH IS AN ENCOMPASSING LIGHT.

Put G‑d's words in your mouth.

THIS IS WHAT YOU DO WHEN YOU LEARN TORAH. G‑D'S BREATH IS YOUR BREATH.

Torah is a gift.

G‑D LOWERS HIMSELF INTO HIS TORAH AND THUS MAKES HIMSELF ACCESSIBLE TO US. WHEN YOU LEARN TORAH, YOUR MIND CONTAINS THE INFINITE WISDOM OF G‑D. IF MOSHE RABBEINU LEARNS TORAH AND A LITTLE CHILD LEARNS TORAH, THERE IS THE SAME AMOUNT OF G‑DLINESS IN THE TORAH THEY LEARN. IT'S JUST THAT MOSHE PERCEIVES MORE OF THE G‑DLINESS.

SURRENDER TO THE

Mitzvahs, Torah Study & Davening.

• TRANSCEND THE FINITE WORLD.
• IS INFINITE LIGHT COMPRESSED SO THAT WE CAN ABSORB IT.
• IS THE G‑DLINESS WE REACH FOR.

WHEN WE DO A MITZVAH, G‑D RAISES US TO HIS LEVEL, AND CONNECTS US TO HIS VERY BEING. OUR SOUL BECOMES ONE WITH G‑D'S LIGHT WHEN WE DO A MITZVAH.

The soul has to rise to the Truth of G‑d.

Level By Level

WE MEET G‑D UP THERE.

Draw down the Infinite Light.

Do a mitzvah Today!

How? Through prayer we become filled with G‑dly Awareness.

PRAYER IS SUPPOSED TO INSPIRE US TO BREAK FREE FROM THE CONSTRICTED LIMITATIONS OF OUR SMALL CONSCIOUSNESS INTO THE HIGHER CONSCIOUSNESS OF G‑DLY AWARENESS. A PERSON WHO ONLY PRAYS BUT DOESN'T LEARN TORAH IS LIKE A PERSON WHO SCREAMS, "I'M THIRSTY!" BUT DOESN'T DRINK THE WATER THAT'S PLACED BEFORE HIM. THROUGH PRAYER WE REFINE OURSELVES TO BE ABLE TO ABSORB THE LIGHT OF TORAH AND SENSE THE G‑DLINESS THAT IS IN THE MITZVAHS WE DO.

IN PRAYER, WE STAND ON OUR TIPTOES AND GIVE G‑D A KISS.

620 WAYS TO ENVELOP OURSELVES IN THE INFINITE LIGHT OF G‑D. (613 PLUS 7 MITZVAHS OF THE RABBONIM).

Sometimes the words let us in.

THEN WE CAN SOAR WITH THE WORDS OF TORAH AND OUR PRAYERS, ESPECIALLY AFTER WE PASS A TEST. BUT EVEN WHEN NOT, THE WORDS STILL MAKE US HOLY.

Torah is G‑d's will to connect to us. Prayer is our desire to connect to G‑d.

TORAH IS G‑D'S WISDOM. MITZVAHS ARE G‑D'S WILL.

Holy Sparks

R. Reuven Wolf   Tanya 5763

☀ HAVE A CONVERSATION WITH G-D ☀

For 5 minutes or more today....,

בס״ד

Talk to G☆d today in the language of your heart.

Holy Sparks
WWW.HOLYSPARKS.COM
© 2017 Rae Shagalov

126

Make this the year you really learn how to pray! בס"ד

Why does prayer work? Because it is a relationship with the Master of the Universe.

Learn how to fight! Learn how to fight evil with your prayers!

It's war!

AND THE WAR IS WITH EVIL AND THE WEAPON IS PRAYER! WE MUST GO TO BOOT CAMP AND LEARN HOW TO PRAY!

YOU HAVE A RELATIONSHIP WITH YOUR CHILD. EVERY DAY YOU SHMOOZE WITH YOUR CHILD. WHEN THE CHILD ASKS YOU FOR MONEY, OF COURSE YOU WANT TO GIVE YOUR CHILD THE MONEY. BUT THE CHILD WHO ONLY CALLS YOU WHEN HE NEEDS MONEY—WHO WANTS TO GIVE HIM MONEY? WHO NEEDS THAT KIND OF RELATIONSHIP?

Prayer is about relationship◆

THE SHUL IS THE PLACE WHERE WE DEVELOP THAT RELATIONSHIP. WHAT KIND OF RELATIONSHIP IS IT WHEN YOU SPEAK OUT YOUR HEART TO YOUR FRIEND AND HE KEEPS LOOKING AT HIS WATCH?!

RABBI YISSACHER FRAND ～∽
TESHUVA DRASHA 5762

UNEDITED NOTES

The more you believe in your prayer, the more real your relationship with G∂d becomes; the more your prayer works!

If you can't pray, then cry!
BECAUSE CRYING IS ALSO PRAYER! CRYING IS THE MOST BASIC PRIMORDIAL EXPRESSION OF THE SOUL. THE NEXT TIME YOU CRY, FOR WHATEVER REASON— USE YOUR TEARS AND SEND THEM UP TO HEAVEN! PRAY WITH YOUR TEARS!

How dare you think your prayer doesn't work! YOU MAY NOT LIVE TO SEE THE RESULTS, BUT THAT DOESN'T MEAN YOUR PRAYERS AREN'T WORKING!

14.74

Holy Sparks

WWW.HOLYSPARKS.COM
© 2017 Rae Shagalov

בס"ד

The Key to the Universe
PRAYER

The world was created so that we should find G‑d in it. How? Through our prayer.

Prayer is not manipulation.

PRAYER IS NOT GETTING G‑D TO DO WHAT WE WANT G‑D TO DO.

How do we pray? FIRST COMES PRAISE, THEN PETITION.

Prayer is talking to the Almighty.

WHY DO WE PRAY? G‑D ALREADY KNOWS WHAT WE NEED. IF IT'S GOOD FOR US, G‑D WILL GRANT IT TO US. IF IT IS NOT GOOD FOR US, WOULD WE REALLY WANT IT ANYWAY? SO, WHY DO WE PRAY?

To reach new heights, To come closer & closer to G‑d.

WE GROW, CHANGE AND IMPROVE THROUGH PRAYER.

Prayer activates our blessings.

The universe is built so that we need G‑d.

G‑d wants the prayers of the righteous.

WHAT IS THE WORST CURSE OF ALL? TO NEVER NEED ANYTHING OR ANYONE.

Prayer connects us to G‑d Through our words.

THE CLOSER WE COME TO G‑D, THE MORE BLESSINGS WE MERIT.

PRAYER PRODUCES RESULTS, NOT BECAUSE G‑D CHANGES, BUT BECAUSE WE CHANGE. WE BECOME HOLIER THROUGH PRAYER.

Prayer brings the blessing down.

All good things, even those things that are meant to happen, will only happen when we unlock the gate that holds them back with the key of our prayer.

Holy Sparks

Rabbi Union "The Art of Prayer"

JEWISH LEARNING EXCHANGE   UNEDITED NOTES

WWW.HOLYSPARKS.COM
© 2017 Rae Shagalov

17.98

בס"ד

Pray!
Empty
the
pockets
of your
Soul

Rebbetzin Esther Jungreis

THINK OF THE GREATNESS OF G-D

ב"ה

Prayer is not about what you get from G-d after you pray, but is about what you get from your prayers while you are praying.

On Shabbos, light the candles, wave the light of Shabbos from the candles into yourself three times, then cover your eyes and remain by the candlelight for a few minutes and talk to G-d.

Think of the greatness of G-d and the smallness of you and that, despite this great difference, G-d is delighted to listen to your prayers.

Thank and praise G-d for every good thing in your life you can remember. Ask G-d for whatever you need, for the needs of each member of your family, for the needs of your friends and the rest of the world.

Ask G-d to be your partner in helping you make those good changes you've started this week. While you are speaking to G-d, feel yourself getting closer to the Master of the Universe, ascending through your prayer.

Melavah Malkah

After You See Three Stars in Different Parts of the Sky on Saturday Night

Make a farbrengen after Havdalah, the ritual for separating the Holy Sabbath from the rest of the week. Record any insights you might have had over Shabbos.

Melavah Malka means "Escorting the Queen." The evening after the Sabbath (Saturday night) is a special spiritual time for the soul to enjoy the lingering holiness of Shabbos and bring it into the week with encouraging words, stories of righteous people (especially the Baal Shem Tov), Torah thoughts and holy songs. It's also customary to have hot drinks (made with fresh water from the faucet) and delicious bread.

ב"ה

Prayer

is the first thing we do each day to bring light into the world.

LIKE THE DAWN, THE LIGHT COMES SLOWLY. THE GEULA COMES SLOWLY, BIT BY BIT. LIKE THE DAWN, THE DARKEST PART OF THE NIGHT COMES JUST BEFORE THE LIGHT.

Prayer

THE TENSION OF THE HEART IS DRAWN TAUT, AND THE HEART'S PRAYER IS RELEASED A GREAT DISTANCE.

Holy Sparks

UNEDITED NOTES

Every moment of our lives, every word can be a prayer.

EVERYTHING WE SAY TO OTHERS, IN OUR FAMILY, IN BUSINESS, IS SCHOOL, IN SHUL, IN OUR COMMUNITY CAN BE ENCOURAGING, CAN BE PRAYERFUL.

Every word of prayer is heard. Every prayer is kept and stored.

NO PRAYER IS EVER WASTED. NEXT WEEK, NEXT YEAR, NEXT GENERATION ～ YOUR PRAYERS WILL HAVE EFFECT.

Rabbi Moshe Teitelbaum

"THE POWER OF TEFILA: IS G·D STILL LISTENING?" ORTHODOX UNION WEST COAST TORAH CONVENTION

→⟫⟫ Gather your family or friends together for a Melavah Malka Farbrengen (Gathering) with a focus of sharing joyful memories and stories. ⟪⟪←

Gather your art supplies and write a decorated letter to G-d. Start with praise and end with thanks. In between, you could include your doubts, needs, fears, regrets, struggles and the things you are trying to improve in your life. If at any time you find yourself at a loss as to what to say to G-d, you can use your letter as a starting place, refining it as you go.

The Finale

⚡ INCREASE YOUR HAPPINESS BY 25% ⚡

Do you want to have a wonderful life? Be thankful!

Gratitude increases joy. The essence of health and wholeness is gratitude. Happiness is a decision you make at the beginning of the day. Look for the good that is in your day — all day long! To be happy is a constant decision. It is training for the reality of the true world, the World to Come.

Who controls your happiness? Your job? Your boss? Your parents? Your spouse? Your children? Your vacation? Your bank account? Happiness is not outside you. Happiness is enjoying what is already in your life. This is training for receiving more.

What you don't have won't make you happy. Only what you do have can make you happy - IF you appreciate what you have. The test is to be grateful, even when thing are difficult -- especially when things are difficult!

G-d gives us the blessings He wants us to have. How can you avoid being frustrated when you don't have what you want? Trust that what you have, you need, and what you don't have, you don't need. We can say we want something, but we cannot say we need it, because if we truly needed it, God would provide it for us.

A study in 2005 found that happiness could be increased by a simple gratitude exercise. Participants took the time to write down 5 things they were grateful for each week, for 10 weeks. At the end of the study this group was 25% happier than a comparison group who simply listed five events from the week. That's it - just five things a week! Surely we can find five things to be grateful for in a whole week. Let's do this!

Be grateful for this moment.

Thank G-d for Everything!

Stop for a moment and look at your life and all your blessings. List everything for which you are grateful, especially the most basic things that perhaps you take for granted such as the breath of life, the ability to move, the delicious flavors of food & scents of flowers, etc.

1.

2.

3.

4.

5.

6.

7.

8.

9.

10.

Find a partner who would like to become 25% happier with you. Once a week, write, email or text each other five things for which you are grateful each week.

Holy Sparks

בס"ד

Thank God for the revealed good and concealed good. THEN WATCH FOR THE MIRACLES IN YOUR LIFE. G♥D PUTS US SOMETIMES IN SITUATIONS WHERE THERE IS NOWHERE TO GO BUT G♥D. WHY? SO WE WILL TURN TO G♥D!

Thank G♥d for the good times. THANK G♥D JOYFULLY IN YOUR QUIET HAPPY MOMENTS; SAY TEHILLIM WHEN ALL IS GOING WELL, AND MAYBE IN THE MERIT OF OUR HAPPINESS AND GRATITUDE, ALL WILL CONTINUE WELL.

The Test IS TO BE GRATEFUL EVEN WHEN THINGS ARE DIFFICULT, ESPECIALLY WHEN THINGS ARE DIFFICULT!

Every moment of my life is a Thank You to Hashem. BEING THANKFUL CREATES A LITTLE BIT OF LIGHT, A CROWN OF SPLENDOR AROUND YOUR HEAD. THE JEWEL OF THE CROWN IS AWE.

Take Nothing for granted. We deserve nothing. It's all a Gift.

תודה

True Thanksgiving is a spontaneous expression that echoes the good that is given to us.

Happiness is not outside you. Happiness is gratitude. HAPPINESS IS ENJOYING WHAT IS ALREADY IN YOUR LIFE. THIS IS TRAINING FOR RECEIVING MORE. WHAT YOU DON'T HAVE WON'T MAKE YOU HAPPY. ONLY WHAT YOU DO HAVE CAN MAKE YOU HAPPY, IF YOU APPRECIATE WHAT YOU HAVE!

Appreciate your life! WITH EVERYTHING YOU ARE! WITH ALL OF YOUR TALENTS! IT'S NEVER TOO LATE TO CHANGE!

Love Hashem twice a day with gratitude. Find five awesome things to be thankful for.

Gratitude makes us a vessel to receive more and more good.

Holy Sparks
WWW.HOLYSPARKS.COM
© 2017 Rae Shagalov

UNEDITED NOTES   TEACHER UNKNOWN

בס"ד

Stay in Joy!

CHOOSE TO FEEL JOY.
VALUE THAT YOU ARE ALIVE.
MAKE A CONSCIOUS CHOICE.

Develop an attitude of gratitude.

APPRECIATE ALL OF
THE PEOPLE AND
THINGS IN YOUR LIFE.

Gratitude makes you want to get up and dance!

WE START OFF WITH
ZERO AND THEN WE
GET LIFE FOR FREE!
GET UP AND
DANCE!

⤜Make a Rosh Chodesh Farbrengen ⤛

⤜❧ CELEBRATE WITH AN UPLIFTING FARBRENGEN WITH FRIENDS ❧⤛

Create a mystical evening of transformation, friendship, story, song and soul with a Rosh Chodesh* farbrengen. Rosh Chodesh means the "head of the month." Rosh Chodesh brings down all of the new spiritual energy for the month during the new moon and is a festive start to the new month.

The Jewish people are compared to the moon. Like the moon, it's our job to light up the darkness and to reflect G-d's light into this world.

A farbrengen is a joyous, inspirational gathering for the purpose of spiritually uplifting the souls of all present. Farbrengens can celebrate a birthday, milestone, yartzeit, or holiday. You can also make a farbrengen when you need a boost of support and spiritual brainstorming to help you elevate a negative experience or get unstuck.

A farbrengen can help you recharge emotionally and spiritually as you benefit from the collective wisdom of your friends. You can strengthen a new resolution by declaring it publicly at the farbrengen and ask your friends to check in with you periodically to see how it's going.

Create an inspiring safe, supportive, non-judgemental, and celebratory santuary with your friends, who want only the best for you. Your friends will help you create a beautiful new canvas for your life, coming from a place of strength, to help you bring out your highest light and holiest actions.

A farbrengen doesn't have to be fancy. Put out some food. Share Torah teachings. Tell chassidic and other inspiring stories. Sing chassidic niggunim or other Jewish songs that uplift the soul. Give and receive blessings for what you need - lots and LOTS of blessings! And make a l'chaim on grape juice, wine or other spirits to raise those blessings even higher.

*Search Chabad.org for more information on Rosh Chodesh and the Jewish months.

It's time for the Breakthrough! בס"ד

Be one with G‑d's Plan for you.

ASK. Receive.

Embrace your Tests.

When you bring G‑d into the picture, everything is different!

May you go Higher & Higher!

It's all from Hashem.

Sometimes, you know it's going to be okay, but you don't know what the okay is going to be.

"I'm here with you. I love you and I'm helping you with this right now," says G‑d

Take some time out to think about what's important to you.

Raise the bar of your faith.

ALWAYS Go after what comes to you.

DON'T LOOK BACK. YOU'LL TURN INTO A PILLAR OF SALT. STUCK.

Farbrengen.

Holy Sparks
WWW.HOLYSPARKS.COM
© 2017 Rae Shagalov

ב"ה

Mazel

COMES FROM THE HEBREW WORD, "TO FLOW DOWN." Mazel is the conduit through which Divine vitality descends upon the person and is then used to accomplish one's mission below.

THE ONLY REASON THAT NEGATIVITY EXISTS IS TO CAUSE AN INCREASE IN HOLINESS AND GOODNESS.

The one who tries to do good is assisted from on High.

Begin Today!

WHY WAIT TO DO GOOD? WHAT WILL YOU DO?

How can you mature in your spiritual growth?

Involve your family in helping you to fulfill your resolutions for good.

By Continually ascending from level to level in all matters of goodness and holiness, more connected to G-d.

THOSE WHO BLESS YOU, WILL BE BLESSED FROM G-D'S FULL, OPEN, HOLY AND BROAD HAND.

• PRAYER • TORAH • MITZVAHS • CHARITY • FARBRENGEN • GATHERING TOGETHER WITH GOOD FRIENDS • IN JOY • WISHING L'CHAIM • • BLESSING EACH OTHER WITH ALL GOOD THINGS •

Put your WHOLE SOUL into it!

HOW WILL YOU BECOME BETTER TODAY THAN YOU WERE YESTERDAY?

You are chosen and special!

Your soul is an actual part of G-d!

Holy Sparks

25 ADAR 5748 • THE BIRTHDAY CAMPAIGN OF THE REBBE •
UNEDITED NOTES   TEACHER UNKNOWN

www.HOLYSPARKS.com
© 2017 Rae Shagalov

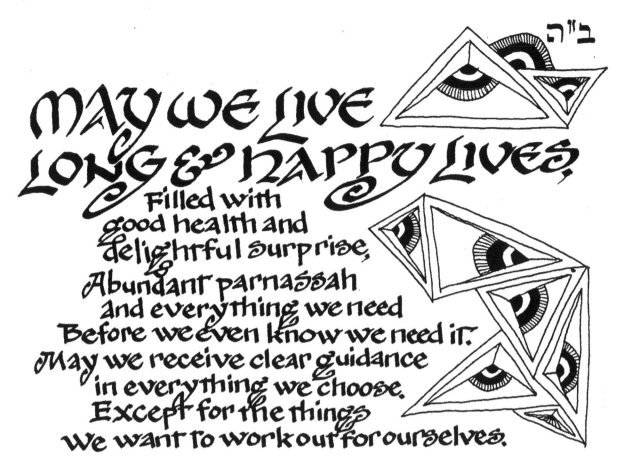

ב"ה

MAY WE LIVE LONG & HAPPY LIVES,
Filled with good health and delightful surprise,
Abundant parnassah and everything we need
Before we even know we need it.
May we receive clear guidance in everything we choose.
Except for the things We want to work out for ourselves.

May we be protected from all manner of distress,
And may the works of our hands & minds
BE BLESSED WITH SUCCESS

May we be and have children who spread mitzvahs like stars, who love and learn Torah for many long years, And may we take all of our days with us.

May we have nachas from ourselves and our loved ones,
AND MAY WE BE A BLESSING TO G‑d!

Holy Sparks

9.38

Farbrengen Notes

The Power of Togetherness

בב"ה

The Farbrengen

IS A HOLY GATHERING FOR CHASSIDIM TO INSPIRE EACH OTHER TO HIGHER LEVELS WITH FOOD, DRINK, STORIES, TORAH, AND NIGUNNIM. @ HOLY MELODIES.

HOLD A FARBRENGEN TO INSPIRE EACH OTHER ON SPECIAL DAYS. @ YOUR BIRTHDAY, HASSIDIC HOLIDAYS. @ ANY TIME YOU OR YOUR FRIENDS NEED SPECIAL ENCOURAGEMENT.

What can we take from this?

ON EVERY JEWISH HOLIDAY AND EVERY HASSIDIC HOLIDAY, WE HAVE TO ASK OURSELVES: WHAT CAN WE LEARN FROM THIS DAY?

THE MESSAGE OF י"ב Tammuz 12 IS:

NEVER GIVE UP!

IT'S NEVER TOO LATE TO BECOME WHAT YOU WANTED TO BE.

It is so important to bless every other Jew.

WHEN WE BLESS EACH OTHER, WE ARE REALLY BLESSING OURSELVES BECAUSE WE ARE ALL CONNECTED.

When you have mesirus nefesh, you *will* succeed!

Mind over Heart

JUST LOOK AT THE FLOURISHING OF JUDAISM IN RUSSIA TODAY!

CHASSIDUS TEACHES US TO BE HAPPY IN OUR SERVICE OF G‑D BY LEARNING TO CONTROL THE EMOTIONS OF THE HEART THROUGH THE SEKHEL, THE INTELLECT.

We are all connected to each other.

WE ARE ONE PEOPLE; IN ISRAEL, WE WERE IN OUR OWN LAND OR IN PROXIMITY TO ONE ANOTHER. THEN WE WERE DISPERSED @ but we are still connected.

"America is no different."

THE PREVIOUS REBBE

THERE WAS YIDDISHKEIT IN THE SHTETYL AND THERE WILL BE YIDDISHKEIT IN AMERICA. HOW? THROUGH ALL JEWS CONNECTING TO ONE ANOTHER AND SHARING THEIR LOVE OF YIDDISHKEIT.

THE HOLY TEMPLES EXISTED TO BRING G‑DLINESS INTO THIS WORLD, AND THIS WORLD EXISTS TO BRING MOSHIACH.

IF WE LEARN THE LAWS OF THE BUILDING OF THE BAIS HAMIKDASH, IT IS AS IF WE ARE BUILDING THE BAIS HAMIKDASH.

5764 Tammuz י"ב

Rabbi Yosef Y. Shagalov

Holy Sparks

WWW.HOLYSPARKS.COM
© 2017 Rae Shagalov

⚜ A NOTE ABOUT G-D* ⚜
WHY SHOULD YOU TALK TO HASHEM?**

There are many benefits to talking to G-d. You will feel calmer and happier when you know that you are not alone. You will increase your faith, improve your character, and have more energy to meet your challenges when you are connected to G-d's infinite source of strength. *Hitbodedut* (meditation) cleanses your soul, connects you to holiness and improves all of your relationships with other people, with yourself, and with G-d.

For best results and a deeper relationship with G-d, make an appointment with Hashem every day. Dedicate a set amount of time each day, and don't let anything stop you! Start with just one minute if you have to, and just show up — even if you don't feel like it or you have nothing to say. By the end of 30 days, you will wonder how you ever lived without talking to G-d every day.

WHY DO WE REFER TO G-D AS "HE"?

Isn't G-d infinitely beyond any gender? Yes, G-d is beyond gender, but we're not. Through the Torah, *Chassidut*, and the mystical *Kabbalah,* we learn the secrets of how G-d created the universe. When they describe the exquisite dance and love relationship between the transcendental and the immanent presence of G-d in this world, the transcendent aspect of the infinite Holy One is presented in the masculine. The immanent divine presence or *Shechinah* and we, who reach for the relationship, are described in the feminine.

----

*To protect G-d's name, we don't spell it out completely. The Jewish people do not write G-d's name in a place where it may be discarded, erased, or carried into an unclean place. Please note that this book should not be taken into a bathroom.

**We often use the Hebrew word "*Hashem*" which means "*The Name*" instead of using G-d's name. Treating G-d's name with this extra reverence is a way to protect the holiness and sanctity of G-d's name.

To learn more about Jewish meditation and get inspired to start a daily practice, you can order Rae Shagalov's beautifully illustrated book, *The Secret Art of Talking to G-d, a 30 Day Creative Prayer Journal of Jewish Meditation* on Amazon at: http://bit.ly/talking-to-G-d

בס״ד

DID YOU MEDITATE TODAY?

Holy Sparks
WWW.HOLYSPARKS.COM
©1990-2016 Rae Shagalov

❧ 10 WAYS TO BE JOYFULLY JEWISH ❧

The most important principle in the Torah is the protection of Jewish life. It's more important than Shabbat, more important than holidays, even fasting on Yom Kippur. Right now, in Israel, and everywhere, Jews must stand together in unity and do whatever possible to protect Jewish life.

The Lubavitcher Rebbe, Rabbi Menachem M. Schneerson, teaches that there are ten important Mitzvahs* we can do to protect life. We urgently need your help to increase in mitzvahs and merits for the Jewish people. Please choose a mitzvah to begin or improve:

1) AHAVAS YISROEL: Behave with love towards another Jew.

2) LEARN TORAH: Join a Torah class.

3) Make sure that Jewish children get a TORAH-TRUE EDUCATION.

4) AFFIX KOSHER MEZUZAS on all doorways of the house.

5) For men and boys over 13: PUT ON TEFILLIN every weekday.

6) GIVE CHARITY.

7) BUY JEWISH HOLY BOOKS and learn them.

8) LIGHT SHABBAT & YOM TOV CANDLES, a Mitzvah for women and girls.

9) Eat and drink only KOSHER FOOD.

10) Observe the laws of JEWISH FAMILY PURITY.

In addition the Rebbe urges that:

Every Jewish man, woman and child should have a letter written for them in a Sefer Torah.**

Every person should study either the Rambam's Yad Hachazakah -Code of Jewish Law or the Rambam's Sefer HaMitzvos.

Concerning Moshiach, the Rebbe stated, "The time for our redemption has arrived!" Everyone should prepare for Moshiach's coming by doing increasing acts of goodness and kindness, and by studying about what the future redemption will be like. May we merit to see the fulfillment of the Rebbe's prophecy. Now!

----

*Mitzvahs are Divine Commandments that connect us to G-d.

**There are several Torah scrolls being written to unite Jewish people and protect Jewish life. Letters for children can be purchased for only $1 via the Internet, at: http://www.kidstorah.org

Listen to inspiring Chassidic Torah classes while you color at:

    Maayon.com   Chabad.org   Torahcafe.com

For more information about how to be Joyfully Jewish, visit:

Holysparks.com	Moshiach.net	Chabad.org	Jewishwoman.org
joyfullyjewish.com	Jewishkids.org	Maayon.com	aish.com
Meaningfullife.com	Inner.org	Breslov.org	torahanytime.com

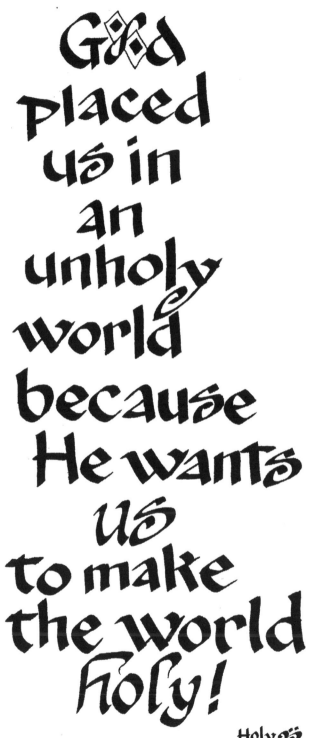

בס"ד

G‑d placed us in an unholy world because He wants us to make the world holy!

Rabbi Reuven Wolf

"The word 'commandment' is a translation of the Hebrew word mitzvah, which also means 'connection.' By observing G-d's commandments, a person becomes connected with G-d's infinite will and wisdom and thereby elicits a G-dly light which shines onto his or her soul.

-Likutei Torah, Rabbi Shneur Zalman of Liadi-

There are seven special mitzvahs, known as the Seven Laws of Noah, which are the minimal Torah observance for non-Jews. The Noahide commandments are those that G-d gave to Adam and his descendants and, after the flood, to Noah and his descendants. They are binding upon all of humanity, and were included in the Torah when G-d gave it to the People of Israel at Mount Sinai. Men and women are equal in their responsibility to observe the Seven Universal Laws.

By learning the Torah laws that pertain to all people and performing these mitzvahs (commandments or Torah laws), the righteous people of all nations help bring this world to a new state of universal holiness, wisdom and peace. "The Seven Noahide Laws" are a sacred inheritance of all the Children of Noah (non-Jews or gentiles), one that every person can use as the basis of his or her spiritual life.

When a gentile resolves to fulfill the Seven Universal Laws, his or her soul is elevated. This person becomes one of the "Chasidei Umot Haolam" (Pious Ones of the Nations) and receives a share of the World to Come.

To Find Out More About the Seven Noahide Laws:
WWW.ASKNOAH.ORG   WWW.NOAHIDE.ORG

❧ THE SEVEN LAWS OF NOAH ❧

Believe in One G-d (Prohibition of Idolatry)

Acknowledge that there is only one G-d who is Infinite and Supreme above all things. Do not replace that Supreme Being with finite idols or other gods.

Keep the Name of G-d Holy (Prohibition of Blasphemy)

Respect the Creator. As frustrated and angry as you may be, don't blame it on G-d Who loves you so much He created you and breathes life into you every moment.

Respect Human Life (Prohibition of Murder)

Human life is holy as man was created in the image of G-d. Every person is of irreplaceable value. Every human being is an entire world, thus to save a life is to save that entire world and to destroy a life is to destroy an entire world.

Respect the Rights & Property of Others (Prohibition of Theft)

Be honest in all your business dealings.
Express your trust in G-d as the Provider of life and your livelihood.

Respect the Family (Prohibition of Illicit Relations)

Respect the institution of marriage. Marriage is a most Divine act. The marriage of a man and a woman is a reflection of the oneness of G-d and His creation. Disloyalty in marriage and other forms of forbidden relationships destroy that oneness.

Respect All Life
(Prohibition of Eating Meat from a Live Animal)

Respect G-d's creatures. At first, Man was forbidden to consume meat. After the Great Flood, he was permitted – but with a warning: Do not cause unnecessary suffering to any creature.

Establish Courts of Justice

Maintain systems of justice. Justice is G-d's business, but we are given the charge to lay down necessary laws and enforce them whenever we can. When we right the wrongs of society, we are acting as partners in creating the perfection of the world.

❧ ABOUT HOLY SPARKS ❧

Holy Sparks is dedicated to spreading the light of authentic Jewish spirituality and wisdom. Holy Sparks provides and promotes Jewish knowledge, awareness and practice as it applies to people of all faiths and nationalities, regardless of affiliation or background. Holy Sparks helps spiritual seekers, particularly the Jewish people, and others who are looking for inspiration and encouragement, to discover and fulfill their individual talents and potential for service to G-d and mankind through increasing in acts of goodness, kindness, and holiness.

❧ ABOUT RAE SHAGALOV ❧

Master calligrapher Rae Shagalov is the author of the Amazon bestseller, *The Secret Art of Talking to G-d,* and the *Joyfully Jewish* series of interactive calligraphy and coloring books for adults and families. Rae is eager to share the beauty and wisdom of Torah through her 3,000 pages of calligraphy Artnotes that reveal the special message of this exciting time in Jewish history.

Rae has combined her experience as a creativity and motivation coach, her talent as a Jewish artist, and her fascinating spiritual search for the true meaning of life to produce these beautiful Jewish Artnotes. Rae's books provide her readers with very practical and creative joy-based action steps for infusing authentic Jewish spirituality into their daily lives. Rae offers Creative Clarity Coaching to help women use their creativity to figure out what they're in this world to do and organize their lives so that they can accomplish it joyfully and creatively. She is also an innovative educator who develops the talents of children through project-based learning at Emek Hebrew Academy in Los Angeles. Find out more about Rae Shagalov's coaching & workshops at: www.holysparks.com.

❧ CONNECT WITH RAE SHAGALOV ❧

Sign up to receive free art, coloring pages and Rae's Soul Tips newsletter! Go to: WWW.HOLYSPARKS.COM

Rae shares art daily on her Facebook page: FACEBOOK.COM/ SOULTIPS

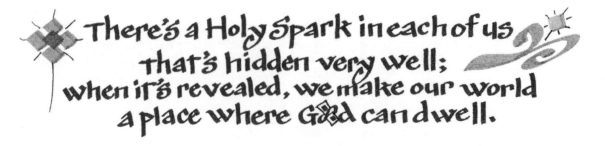
There's a Holy Spark in each of us that's hidden very well; when it's revealed, we make our world a place where G-d can dwell.

CREATIVE WORKSHOPS, ART SHOWS & AUTHOR TOURS
ARE YOU LOOKING FOR A TRULY UNIQUE, FUN AND INSPIRING EVENT?

- Book-Signing Events & Art Shows
- Inspiring & creative Joyfully Jewish workshops
- Birthday Farbrengens for you, your group, or someone you want to honor
- Rosh Chodesh Women's Events

"The women loved it!"
~Mrs. Sara Labkowski, Director, Machon Chana

"I felt acceptance, warmth, guidance, friendship and sisterhood in the Joyfully Jewish workshop."

"Every minute of the workshop was joyful and insightful."

"Creating with other Jewish women is awesome. I realized we have so much in common in our journeys."

Sign up to get on the mailing list to find out about future events at: WWW.HOLYSPARKS.COM

Calligraphy Commisions, Dedications, & Sponsorships

- Sponsor or dedicate a book or page in honor or memory of someone special.
- Commission new art, books or videos.

Contact Rae Shagalov
info@holysparks.com

Creative Clarity Coaching

- Work with Rae to clarify your life purpose, create strategies to overcome a challenge, jumpstart your creativity, or plan a new project.
- Guide your team's creative project with memorable calligraphic recording.

Interviews
Would you like to interview Rae or feature her art, videos or articles in your magazine, newspaper, blog, podcast or website?

Press Kit Here:
HOLYSPARKS.COM/PAGES/PRESS

✦ CLAIM YOUR FREE BONUS! ✦

Be sure to claim your bonus. As a thank-you for purchasing this book, I have a free gift for you that includes a bonus Soul Adventure and coloring page for you to print and enjoy. Be sure to sign up for your gift bonus at:

holysparks.com/pages/Joy1

✦ MY DEEP APPRECIATION & GRATITIUDE ✦

I am deeply grateful to my coaching clients who helped me
develop this workbook and the Joyfully Jewish Workshops through their
deep quest for their creative expression and spiritual truth,
to Shimona Tzukernik for helping me develop outreach for this book
and to my dear husband Rabbi Yosef Yitzchok for his help with *everything!*

LET'S CONNECT!
Facebook.com/soultips
Pinterest.com/holysparks
Twitter.com/holysparks
Youtube.com/holysparksbooks
Instagram.com/holysparks

I would love to hear your insights and questions and see your colorful creations, so let's connect! Feel free to email me with questions, suggestions & pictures of your coloring at: INFO@HOLYSPARKS.COM

Sign up to receive free art & coloring pages
and Rae Shagalov's Joyfully Jewish Artnotes Newsletter!
Go to: www.holysparks.com

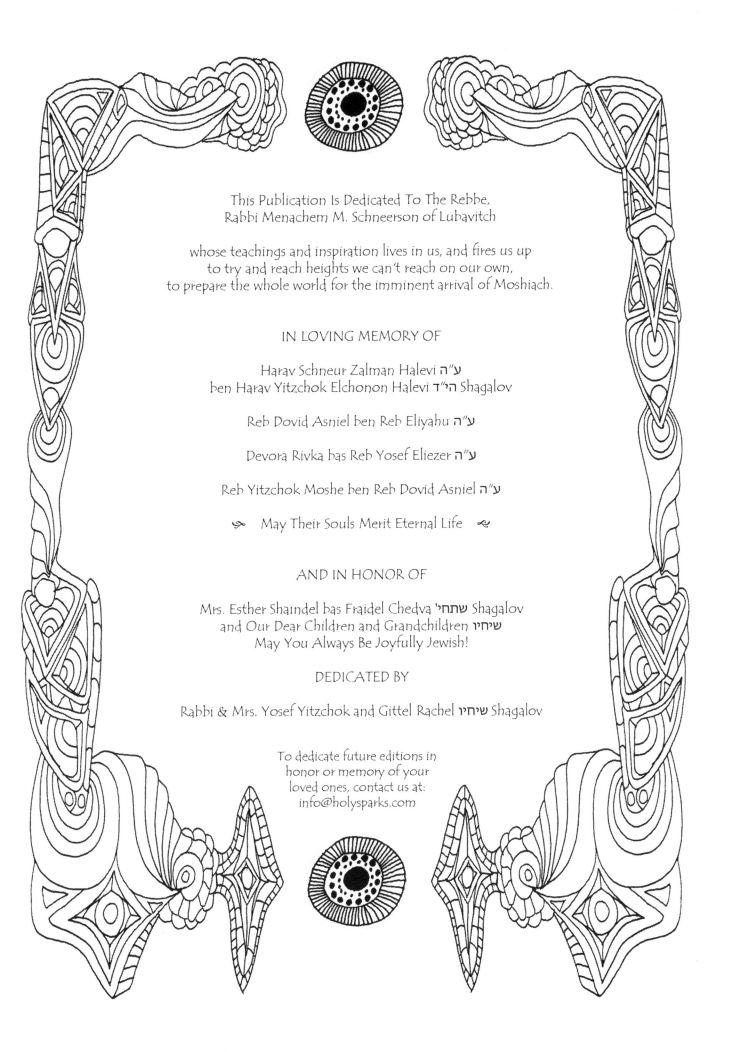

This Publication Is Dedicated To The Rebbe,
Rabbi Menachem M. Schneerson of Lubavitch

whose teachings and inspiration lives in us, and fires us up
to try and reach heights we can't reach on our own,
to prepare the whole world for the imminent arrival of Moshiach.

IN LOVING MEMORY OF

Harav Schneur Zalman Halevi ע״ה
ben Harav Yitzchok Elchonon Halevi הי״ד Shagalov

Reb Dovid Asniel ben Reb Eliyahu ע״ה

Devora Rivka bas Reb Yosef Eliezer ע״ה

Reb Yitzchok Moshe ben Reb Dovid Asniel ע״ה

❧ May Their Souls Merit Eternal Life ☙

AND IN HONOR OF

Mrs. Esther Shaindel bas Fraidel Chedva שתחי׳ Shagalov
and Our Dear Children and Grandchildren שיחיו
May You Always Be Joyfully Jewish!

DEDICATED BY

Rabbi & Mrs. Yosef Yitzchok and Gittel Rachel שיחיו Shagalov

To dedicate future editions in
honor or memory of your
loved ones, contact us at:
info@holysparks.com

❧ GLOSSARY ❧

Aramaic:	The vernacular of Jews in the Land of Israel in the first century, used in some texts and prayers, such as Kaddish
Ahavas Yisrael:	Love for a fellow Jew
Amalek:	An enemy of the Jews, recurring throughout the generations; the embodiment of evil and doubt
Amen:	"So be it;" an affirming response to a blessing
Baal Shem Tov:	Rabbi Yisroel ben Eliezer (born circa 1700, died 22 May 1760), founder of the Chassidic Judasim
Bashert:	Meant to be; sent from G-d
Bais/Beis Hamikdash:	The Holy Temple
Bina:	Understanding
Bitachon:	Trust in G-d
Brachas/Brachot	Blessings
Chochma:	Wisdom
Chassid:	A follower of a Chassidic Rebbe who lives according to Chassidic principles and practices
Chassidic:	A branch of Orthodox Judaism founded in 18th-century Eastern Europe by Rabbi Israel Baal Shem Tov, based on spiritual re-awakening through Torah, mysticism and Ahavas Yisrael.
Cheshbon HaNefesh:	Introspection; literally, "Accounting of the Soul"
Chesed:	The quality of lovingkindness
Choson/Chossan:	Bridegroom
Daled:	The 4th letter in the Hebrew alphabet with a "d" sound
Daas:	Knowledge
Davenning:	Praying
Eliahu Hanavi:	Elijah the Prophet
Emunah:	Faith
Farbrengen:	A joyous gathering for the participants to encourage each other in Torah learning, the fulfillment of the Mitzvot, and the spreading of Yiddishkeit (Judaism)
Gan Eden:	The Garden of Eden
Gemarah:	The collection of Rabbinic writings constituting the basis of religious authority in Torah law
Gentiles:	Non-Jewish people
Geulah:	The Messianic Era, a time of universal peace and the revelation of G-dliness, which will be ushered in by a Jewish leader generally referred to as the Moshiach
Gevurah:	The quality of severity, limitation
Galus/Golus:	Exile from G-dliness

Hakodesh Baruch Hu: The Blessed Holy One

Hashem: G-d; literally, "The Name"

Hitbodedut: Self-isolation or seclusion; the Jewish meditation practice of speaking privately with G-d.

Kabbalah: "Tradition," the general term for Jewish mysticism. Authentic Jewish mysticism is an integral part of Torah.

Kavanah: Intent, concentration

Kavod: Honor and respect

Kishkes: Literally means intestines or guts as in a "gut feeling"

Klal Yisrael: The collective body of the Jewish people

Klippah: An evil shell (so to speak) that obstructs holiness

Kodesh, Kedushah: Holy or holiness; to separate and sanctify what is G-dly from what comes from the opposite of G-dliness or holiness

Kohen: A member of the priestly tribe of the Jewish people

Kohen Gadol: The High Priest who served in the Holy Temple in Jerusalem

Kvetch: To complain

Lashon Hara: Gossip, evil speech

L'Chaim: "To life;" a traditional Jewish toast and blessing

Malach: An angel

Malchus: The quality of royalty

Maimonides: Moses Maimonides, also known as the Rambam, one of the greatest Jewish scholars

Melava Malka: "Escorting the Queen." A traditional Saturday night meal following Shabbat with bread, stories, and songs

Messiah: See Moshiach

Messianic Era: See Geulah

Mensch: A good and trustworthy person of integrity

Mesirus Nefesh: Self-sacrifice

Minyan: A quorum of 10 men over the age of 13, required for traditional Jewish public worship

Mishegass: Foolishness

Mishkan: Tabernacle

Moshiach: The Anointed Redeemer, Messiah who in the time of Redemption will rebuild the Holy Temple in Jerusalem, gather the Jewish people from around the world and return them to the Promised Land.

Mitzvahs or Mitzvot: Commandments (that connect us to G-d)

Moshe Rabbeinu: Moses

Nachas: Yiddish for pride and joy, especially when children live a Torah life.

N'aseh v'Nishmah: "To do and to hear;" the Jewish people accepted the mitzvahs at Mt. Sinai unconditionally

153

Niggun/Nigunnim:	Transcendental Chassidic songs
Nun:	A Hebrew letter with the "n" sound
Parnassah:	Livelihood
Pintele Yid:	Essential Jewishness
Ra:	Evil
Rambam:	See Maimonides
Ribono Shel Olam:	Master of the Universe
Ruach:	Spirit; one of the levels of the soul
Sekhel:	Intellect
Shabbos/Shabbat:	The Sabbath day of rest
Shalom Bayis:	A peaceful home
Shechina:	The Divine Presence as it manifests in this world
Simcha:	Happiness, joy
Shlemazel:	An unlucky, hapless person
Shmooze:	To chat
Shmutz:	Filth
Shtetyl:	A Jewish village
Shul:	Synagogue
Tammuz:	The fourth month of the Hebrew calendar
Teferes/Teferet:	The soul's quality of beauty, harmony, balance
Tefillah:	Prayer
Tefillin:	Two small leather boxes attached to straps that contain four sections of the Torah inscribed on parchment used for a mitzvah
Tehillim/Psalms:	The book of 150 songs and praises of G-d by King David
Teshuva:	Repentance; returning to the righteous path of Torah and G-d
Torah:	The Five Books of Moses; the entire body of Jewish knowledge; G-d's thought and will condensed in a physical scroll
Tumah:	Impurity
Tzaddik:	A pious, saintly man
Tzedakah:	Charity
Tzimtzum:	In Jewish mysticism, the process whereby G-d concealed Himself in order to create this world with free choice
Tzitzit/Tzitzis	A fringed, 4-cornered undergarment worn to fulfill a mitzvah
Yartzeit:	Anniversary of a person's death
Yetzer Hara:	The urge to do wrong
Yetzer Tov:	The urge to do what is good and right
Yiddishkeit:	Judaism
Zohar:	A commentary on the Torah which is a central mystical work of Jewish mysticism

INDEX OF SOUL ADVENTURES

WILL YOU BE KIND ENOUGH
TO DO ME A FAVOR?

Have you found anything in this book that was enjoyable or useful to you?
Did you learn anything new or change for the better in any way?
Did anything particularly inspire you or increase your joy?
Or maybe you would just like to say, "Thank You!"

Please leave a review on Amazon!
Here's the link to find this and all of my other books on Amazon:
http://amzn.to/2ayKVET

It would be very helpful for me, as well as those who are considering whether or not to buy *Joyfully Jewish* for their own personal growth or to give as a gift to a friend if you would kindly leave a review for the book on Amazon. This will help us reach many more people with this Jewish wisdom that is especially for our generation to prepare the world for Moshiach. Thank you so much!

COLOPHON

The Artnotes in this book were all originally handwritten and drawn during classes. The Headings are Felix Titling and the main printed text is the Catalina font family. Other fun fonts include: Amorie, Angelia, Avaline, Before Breakfast, Black & White, Jamie Woods, Mystiqe, Readmitted, Ginger Snap, Love Mile, July Kissed, Patrick Handletter, Rivina, Sweet September, Tempus Sans, & True Sketch. Some of the coloring pages were digitally modified from the original Artnotes using Repper Pro.

Look for More Interactive Calligraphy Books
By Rae Shagalov on amazon.com

The Secret Art of Talking to G-d

30 Different Ways to Get Closer to G-d!
Start or deepen your meditation with this step-by-step program for 30 days to help create or renew your relationship with G-d! Filled with beautiful full color art & calligraphy and 30 meditation and journal prompts for exploring your relationship with G-d.

You already talk to G-d?
Great! You will love that each Soul Adventure focuses on a unique theme to help you develop the nuances of your soul and deepen your relationship with G-d.

Never tried to talk to G-d before?
The meditation adventures in this Soul Journey will guide you through a magnificent inner journey into your own soul where your finite, limited self merges with the infinite, majestic strength and comfort of the Master of the Universe.

"I decided to read one 'Soul Adventure' a day. Each Soul Adventure is short and simple, but enough for you to work with. It gives you a lot to think about throughout your day. I've found them meaningful, inspirational and motivating. Even though this book is geared towards the Jewish faith I think that anyone can benefit from it."
-Shoshana Michel-

"Such beautiful, uplifting wisdom! I keep buying more of these to give out to my friends." -A.N.M.-

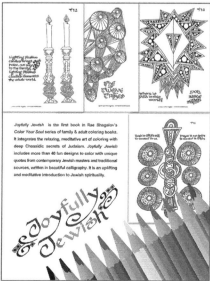

Joyfully Jewish
Family & Adult Coloring Book

"I was thrilled to see that "adult" coloring books are "in" but I wanted something Jewish!!! I couldn't believe my eyes when I saw Rae's book...and then I was even more excited to receive it and see that it's not only full of cool things to color.....each page is a whole "lesson" for a JOYFUL JEWISH LIFE!!! I can't wait to give them to friends, family, and of course, to get coloring!!!!"
-Malka Forshner-

Notes

בס"ד

Holy Sparks
www.HOLYSPARKS.COM
© 2017 Rae Shagalov

Made in the USA
Las Vegas, NV
25 January 2024

84886310R10087